what Buddhism can offer

a path for parents

Sara Burns

windhorse publications

Published by
Windhorse Publications Ltd
11 Park Road
Birmingham
B13 8AB
United Kingdom

Cover artwork: Debbie Harter
Cover design: Marlene Eltschig
Printed by Cromwell Press Ltd, Trowbridge, England

A catalogue record for this book is available from the British Library
ISBN: 978 1 899579 70 9

contents

for Jai and Ella
with love

acknowledgements

I would like to thank the more than two dozen (mainly) Buddhist parents who met me, were interviewed over the telephone, came to group discussions, and/or shared their talks or articles about Buddhism and parenting. The material for this book has been developed from their stories and experiences combined with my own.

Thank you therefore to Amaragita, Bodhakari, Devapriya, Jayagita, Kulamitra, Santva, Subhamayi, Sugati, Vagisvari, Vajrin, Vijayasri, Denise Dobson, Melodie Holliday, Joy MacKeith, Margo Messenger, Lesley Williams, Kathy Roberts, Alistair, Dawn, Jacqui, Julie, Rebecca, Terry, and others who have participated in the discussions. I learned an enormous amount through talking to them and was often very moved and inspired. I have drawn from much of this inspiration in my own life as well as for this book. Special mention goes to Punyamala, Sadara, and Vajrapushpa, as I repeatedly found myself drawing on their experiences.

I also want to thank Maitreyi who helped plant the idea in my mind in the first place, and for one particularly inspiring talk which helped me understand and write about the need to separate pain from blame within the context of forgiveness. And Parami, for recognizing my spiritual practice, being my friend and mentor, her confidence in my ability to write a book, and for many teachings, including a powerful talk on responding to suffering with love.

Thank you, too, to my parents, Paul and Penny Burns, who made a pretty good job of raising me, which left me with the freedom and confidence to travel and explore, spiritually and in other ways, sharing little of the anxiety they must have felt as I wandered Latin America alone, for example. Their acceptance and support of the life changes I made along the way, including Buddhist ordination, has been really important to me. I particularly appreciate my mother's many expressions of confidence in me as a parent, which have been so immensely helpful in enabling me to learn how to be one – something I am still learning.

I also want to thank my work partners in Triangle Consulting, Joy MacKeith and Kate Graham, who are also working mothers. They have been positive, reassuring, and encouraging throughout, often saying a very important 'well done' and reminding me when I fretted over my lack of productivity that it was no mean feat to write a book alongside work and motherhood.

A special thank you to Martha Rios-Lopez (Akasavajri), who lived with me and my children for a lot of the time I researched and wrote this book, and was the only person who read each chapter as I went along – the only person I trusted to read early drafts. As well as providing me with just the right reference or text from an extensive Buddhist library, we had many stimulating, animated, and enjoyable discussions, which were enormously helpful in working out what I wanted to say.

Thank you also to Debbie Harter, my cousin, for designing exactly the cover illustration that I wanted at very short notice. Debbie and I shared a great deal of our childhood and adolescence, and having her design the cover picture has meant a lot to me.

Finally, thank you to everyone at Windhorse Publications, particularly Jnanasiddhi, who really is extremely good at her job. My impression is that since the first impartial and inadequate draft of this book, I have simply followed Jnanasiddhi's advice and it has worked, first to steep myself in the subject of each chapter in turn, to find my own voice, and later providing clear advice on the polishing stage. I have learned a great deal along the way.

Thank you all!

about the author

Sara Burns was born in 1962, the second of four children, and spent her early childhood in Barnes, London. When she was 11 the family moved to a tiny Somerset village, where her parents still live. She was raised a Catholic, attended a convent secondary school, and became a regular member of the local church congregation.

In 1985, after university and two years working in market research, Latin America became an important part of her life for over a decade, where she travelled, got involved in the human rights movement, and worked in the Latin America section of a UK development agency. She continued to travel after her first child was born in 1994, but this phase ended with the birth of her second child in 1996.

Sara first came across Buddhism in Nepal in 1990, and then became involved in the establishment of the North London Buddhist Centre in the early 1990s. She was ordained within the Western Buddhist Order in 2005 and given the name Karunagita, which means 'song of compassion'. She regularly gives talks and leads events around the theme of parenting and Buddhism and other topics.

Since 1998, Sara has raised her children largely on her own and has worked as a consultant for a range of charities and voluntary organizations, joining forces with two other women in 2003 to set up a partnership. This is her first book – but it is not intended to be her last. She currently lives in North London with her two children.

introduction

my story

I never meant to be a Buddhist. It crept up on me over a great many years. There was no inkling of any such tendency as an extremely conventional teenager. Later, I had a shy fascination when anyone mentioned meditation and, by my mid-twenties, a vague underlying sense of searching and not fitting in, but none of my friends meditated or talked of things spiritual. It was not until I first travelled to the East that I felt free to try meditation myself, less self-conscious in the land I associated with meditation and far from those who knew me. I learned to meditate on a short Buddhist retreat in Nepal in 1990. I loved it straight away, and I felt bigger, happier, and bursting with energy by the end. The image I used at the time was that I had been plugged into the mains, filled with electricity, and given a battery-charger to take home with me, in the form of meditation.

By the time my first child was born in May 1994, meditation and other activities at my local Buddhist centre, and going on three or four retreats a year, were my priority. After Jai's birth, I still went to my weekly evening class at the Buddhist centre and made space to meditate most days. This was at the expense of things that other people do with small windows of quiet and opportunity in the early years of parenting, such as sleep, eat, wash up, or have an uninterrupted conversation. When the baby slept, I meditated. I swapped baby-sitting with other parents to gain a couple of child-free hours here and there, and I was able to go on a week-long retreat when my son was eighteen months old. I carved out time from my life as a working mother to practise Buddhism. However, if my son woke unexpectedly or anything else got in the way, I often felt frustrated or became resentful. I quickly became oppressed by my life, kicking against what I saw as a lack of space for spiritual practice. I went on in that way for about two and a half years.

It was not until a couple of months after my daughter was born that a shift occurred, somewhere deep in my body. The thought that surfaced in my mind was, 'I no longer have time to step out of my life to practise Buddhism, so I'll just have to bring Buddhism into my life.' At the time, it felt more like resignation and acceptance of a practical alternative than the moment of epiphany I now see it as, but it was a turning point. Obvious as it may have seemed to others all along, that, for me, was the start of trying to live my life as my spiritual practice, rather than walking away from my day-to-day life and the people in it in order to be 'spiritual'.

For a great many years – at least ten – I believed it was possible to lead a rich and positive spiritual life in the context of raising children, but I was unable to articulate *how*, or to have such conversations with others easily. The way I see it, parenting is not inherently spiritual, any more than the lifestyles of non-parents, or other things we devote our time and energy to; we do not develop spiritually simply by being parents. The world would be a very different place if we did. It is usually hard to find calm or space within a family life, yet for many years I have had an underlying confidence that raising children is full of opportunities to grow as our children grow. A thread running through my life has been working out how to do that. This book is an important part of that ongoing exploration.

this book

So how do we lead rich and meaningful spiritual lives in the context of parenting? What is this wealth of opportunities, and how can parents make best use of them? Are there ways to approach the difficulties or potential pitfalls? How can we help ourselves through the difficult times and stay true to the wisdom and compassion we are trying to bring into our lives? Are there practical techniques on which we can draw? How can we understand our everyday experience in the context of our spiritual aspirations?

These are some of the questions this book aims to answer. The emphasis is on 'how'. It is intended to be practical and helpful. This book is for anyone exploring what it means to develop their spiritual life within the context of raising children. This includes Buddhists, people interested in exploring Buddhism, those involved in other spiritual or religious traditions, and people starting an open exploration of what spirituality means for them. I have drawn on Buddhist teachings to answer these questions, but you do not need to know anything about Buddhism to understand them. There is no Buddhist jargon and most of the teachings are of universal relevance. I hope the book will also be of value to Buddhist teachers and others who are supporting parents on a spiritual path.

This book is *not* about how to be a good parent, how to raise happy children, or how to provide children with a spiritual context. There are numerous books on these subjects, and I feel far from qualified to write one. However, this book *is* written in the belief that our spiritual growth can only have a positive effect on our children.

In developing the material for this book I have drawn on my own experiences and that of over two dozen other (mainly) Buddhists parents living in the UK. With a few exceptions, they are all members of the community of Buddhists called the Friends of the Western Buddhist Order.

Although the majority are mothers, white, and married or in heterosexual partnerships, a significant minority were from black or minority ethnic backgrounds, gay, single, or fathers. They also include people with very different levels of experience of Buddhism. Many have one, two, or even three decades of Buddhist spiritual practice behind them and were already practising Buddhists when they became parents. Others came across Buddhism relatively recently. Some have babies and young children, others were coping with teenagers and exam times, and a few were grand-parents.

In talking with this wide range of individuals, certain themes repeated and resonated with my own experience. It is these themes that make up this book. However, I have relied a great deal on my own experience, so many of the stories are about my response to situations with my own children, Jai and Ella. What clearly emerges is that my first born, Jai, has presented me with the most challenges, and has had the most to teach me, and I have draw on this ex-perience in many stories, especially those associated with self-awareness and patience! By the time my second child arrived, I had learned and moved on, and things were eas-ier. Ella appears more in the stories about fun, fearlessness, and ethics. But both my children have taught me a huge amount within all the themes.

Jai and Ella are now 12 and 10 respectively. I have talked with both of them about this book and about the stories that involve them. I was prepared to change anything they were not happy about, but I am pleased and grateful that I didn't need to do that. Jai had a very positive response to some of the more difficult issues, and said, 'You've got to tell it like it is.' On the whole, both children were pleased to have a book written about them! However, one area that does lose out within this book is that of both parents (or a parent and step-parent) living together to raise children, including mutual support and the ongoing need to negotiate and agree. I separated from Jai and Ella's father while Ella was still a toddler and, although I am in a relationship, that is not an area I feel qualified to write about.

I have learned an enormous amount while researching and writing this book, especially the powerful effect of awareness. Even if the words and concepts are not new, the process of simply paying attention to each theme can transform our experience, especially in the context of our spiritual aspirations. While developing the chapter on love and letting go, I lived with a joyous open heart, totally in love with my children and appreciative, grateful, and loving towards everyone around me and beyond. Writing about ethics, I lived with a sense of clarity and gratitude for Buddhist teachings on forgiveness and the Buddhist principles of ethical behaviour. The process of writing also made me much more aware and appreciative of the opportunities for reflection that come our way as parents. And I thoroughly enjoyed singing the praises of family life as a way to help us live our lives more fully, embracing opportunities and each other and learning from our children about the wonders of the moment. I hope this book will fuel you with confidence, understanding, love, and enthusiasm for the path ahead, as it has for me.

spiritual aspiration

You may have picked up this book because you are have a spiritual aspiration, perhaps a heartfelt longing to connect with something higher than yourself. Much of this book is about how to maintain that aspiration, connecting with love, compassion, and understanding to transform our experience of daily life and enable us to grow through the tasks involved in raising children. We are trying not to separate 'spiritual' aspects of ourselves or activities from the day-to-day realities of raising children, housework, and earning a living. After all, if we don't explore, honour, and live our spiritual connections and aspirations now, when will we do so? Can it really wait until we have more time on our hands?

Throughout the book, I have suggested how we can bring awareness into each moment, reflect, and maintain our connection with our aspirations in different situations. The concluding chapter includes a brief round-up of some of the tools we can use to help us develop awareness. Below are a few practical things you can do to help keep your connection with your aspirations alive. You may have ideas of your own ideas already.

aspirations in the kitchen and beyond
Quotations on the fridge or kitchen wall is one technique. A friend of mine has one that reads, 'Happiness is not doing what you want to do, it is enjoying what you do.' This is a gentle reminder of the need to find satisfaction in what we find ourselves doing and to connect more areas of our lives to our spiritual practice.

Another friend realized that having children challenged her patience, and found that responding to them with kindness instead of impatience had an immediate effect on her and the children. To remind her of this. she had a quotation from the Buddha on her kitchen wall: 'Patience is the greatest asceticism,' (meaning that it is the greatest of all spiritual practices).

One Buddhist mother created a shrine box for her vegetable knife – a shrine to the Buddhist archetypal figure of infinite love, with a slot for her knife. Cooking is something she enjoys and considered important in terms of her family sitting down to eat together. The box was her reminder to connect with loving-kindness every time she picked up the knife.

Someone else I interviewed stressed the importance of a 'daily do' to keep us in contact with our higher selves and our aspiration. This could be some form of ritual or silence, for example, even for only for a minute or two, or lighting a candle, or looking at an image that is meaningful to you.

On the wall next to my kettle I have two photographs taken in a wood one summer evening. They remind me to stop, breathe, and feel the ground under my feet while waiting for the kettle to boil, instead of mindlessly snacking from nearby jars – a habit I can easily slip into. They remind me of stopping and breathing when I felt spacious and calm, pausing to look up at the sky, stroking the twists of hawthorn branches, and the grounding effect of ancient trees and nourishing greenery, of feeling centred and present – how I want to feel all the time.

1

love and letting go

Even as a mother protects with her life
Her child, her only child,
So with a boundless heart
Should one cherish all living beings;
Radiating kindness over the entire world:
Spreading upward to the skies,
And downward to the depths;
Outward and unbounded,
Freed from hatred and ill-will. [1]

Have you ever really enjoyed being with someone – a friend, a baby, a lover perhaps, or even on your own, enjoying a beautiful view or some music – when suddenly you became aware of enjoying yourself, feeling happy, maybe even full of love, lightness, or joy? You might even have been conscious of wanting nothing else in that moment. But then a little fearful thought creeps in, something like, 'I don't want this to end,' or 'What if I lose him/her?' And bang, the sense of complete happiness disappears.

It has often happened to me. I become aware of feeling happy, and then, involuntarily, wanting to hold on to that moment. Of course I know it can't last for ever, but I want it to last just a little longer. And in that wanting, the intensity of pleasure inevitably fades and some pain creeps in. Buddhism emphasizes this inability to hold on to anyone or anything. We cannot fix it in time, yet that is exactly what we often try to do. Everything and everyone changes, whether from moment to moment or gradually, over time. We cannot depend on anyone or anything to stay with us or stay the same for ever – or even just as long as we want it to. If our happiness depends on just that, it will be a fragile and vulnerable happiness. I want to be able to enjoy and love without holding on – to kiss the joy as it flies – either free of, or embracing, my fear of losing that which I love. We may know this truth in our heads, but it is a different matter to know it in our guts. This is, as they say, easier said than done.

One father I spoke to told me that his life began when his son was born. When I asked what it was that started, he paused briefly and then replied, 'my heart'. His heart opened and he found himself living each day with far more intensity than he had lived since childhood. His life before the arrival of his son, and all his previous experience of love, suddenly paled in comparison to what he now felt. He became aware of bits of himself, such as his desire to cherish and nurture, that he had not used before, or not since he looked after his pets as a small child. Throughout the process of researching this book, I was moved by listening to parents talk about the heart opening, and the love they experienced that rendered all other love weak by comparison. Yet from the moment they first walk, or even before, our children start to move away from us, to look elsewhere in order to reveal themselves as individuals. That they change is perhaps the one thing we can rely on. Letting them go is unavoidable. There is no way we can hold on to them – yet we cannot imagine not having them so constantly in our lives.

Loving and letting go is the fundamental nature of all our relationships. Within both the loving and the letting go lie some of the great gifts of parenting and opportunities for spiritual growth. In the *Metta Sutta*, quoted above, the Buddha drew on the love of a mother for her child to emphasize and illustrate a 'boundless heart'. Our human

9

capacity for love is, he taught, unbounded. This is quite a thought: that as human beings we have the capacity to feel for all living beings the intensity of love a parent feels for their child. We can learn, bit by bit, day by day, to radiate kindness, to be confident in our capacity to love, to learn to love with our hands open, letting go with awareness, until we have a boundless heart. Along the way we cannot but grow spiritually and have a positive effect on the world around us and, of course, the children we are raising.

the gift of love

When Jai was born, I remember holding him in my hands, looking at his face and his tiny fingers, and reeling with the sheer force of protective love that hit and then over-whelmed me, bringing tears to my eyes. I was completely unprepared for the strength of this feeling. I was a mother lion, with gruesome images of ripping someone to pieces with my teeth or bare hands should they threaten his safety. Many other mothers and fathers have talked and written about these unfamiliar new feelings, and the effect of suddenly loving with such intensity. Parents' love for their children can contain so many strands of emotion: deep, raw, unconditional love; fear and anxiety about loss or what might happen to their children; pride; the desire to care, protect, and nurture; and a deep feeling of connection with another human being.

But love is not confined to those individuals we are linked to by blood. Love is also the nature of the universe, the nat-ural order of things, that which is beyond and bigger than ourselves, whether we are in touch with it or not. It is not just something personal, generated within us by contact with particular individuals or limited by what we see as our individual capacity to love. One image that comes to mind is a stream of positive energy – love – that flows around us all the time. It is up to me to remember it is there and con-nect with it. Sometimes I just dip in my toe, but at other times I can let go, lie back, and allow myself to be supported, buoyed up, or carried by it, trusting my intuition and having faith that, when I am in touch with that energy, I will make the right choices. From the glimpses I have, I can see that the boundless heart of which the Buddha spoke is contacted by opening and trusting, resting in the natural order of things; it is contacted by opening my heart. I want to live my life with that kind of faith, trusting that buoyancy. But I keep losing touch with it in the busyness of life, various forces pulling me in different directions, and in the resulting tiredness.

My day-to-day experience is that I am often with other people, but there is a level on which I feel separate from them. I want more real connections with friends and family, and to love more fully, but I hold back. You may have a similar experience. Have you ever felt sad and in need of comfort, but actually retreated, unable to face the world? Or felt happy yet wanted to give a wide berth to friends or colleagues who are habitually negative or going through a hard time? Our fear that their difficulties or complaints might rub off on us and cause our own precious happiness to end can make us close down to them or to other possible threats around us.

We might have a similar response when hearing news of suffering in distant parts of the world. In these situations, our heart does not feel boundless. Why do we do this? Buddhism teaches us that, somewhere along the line, we have come to see ourselves as separate individuals. We lose sight of our connections with life, and this is why we behave as we do. We may crave love and support in times of difficulty, or long to radiate and share our happiness, but, failing to see our connections with others, we build barriers. We think we will feel safer by closing our hearts, but with that comes a shutting down of our experience.

Although having children can help break down these barriers, this is not always the case. Not all parents fall in love with their children at birth. I read somewhere that about a third of parents fall head-over-heels in love with their baby. For others, love may take time to develop or might always be a struggle. One mother I spoke to had found the early years of parenting mostly hard, alone with her baby. It was only when her daughter started school that she had her most direct experience of her capacity to love. Her daughter settled easily and was happy at school, leaving her free from the anxiety of leaving a child who did not want to be left. Her quality of life seemed to improve instantly by having more space and freedom. Then, on separating from her daughter at school one morning, she felt her heart suddenly open with immense love, together with an exquisite and almost unbearable pain. This gave her a glimpse of what is meant by a boundless heart and her capacity for love.

This intensity of love is not a constant experience for any of us; at best, it may be fleeting or sporadic. Another aspect of this love for our children is that it keeps challenging us to be there for another human being who may rarely, if ever, tell us how grateful they are, who pushes us to our limits, and even defies our attempts to do what is good for them. In other words, being a parent challenges us to love unconditionally, not dependent on what the loved one does or says. Although we may argue with our children, feel deep frustration, irritation, anger, even dislike or hatred, we aim to love them through it all. And this can teach us so much about our hearts and offer insight into our potential and capacity to love, care for, and protect other beings.

The Buddha taught that we are not separate, but intimately connected to each other and the world in which we live, in so many ways. If you think for a moment, you can easily identify ways in which you have an effect on others, or they on you. You might consider the world's resources and the people needed to keep you and your family alive day by day; all the ways in which you know you are not really separate. Yet to react and behave as though we are separate from others is deeply ingrained, and it is this very illusion of separation that causes us pain and isolation. To really feel our boundless heart we need to keep chipping away at this sense of ourselves as separate. That is another reason why love for our children is a gift. As parents, we connect deeply with at least one other human being, not holding ourselves separate. To me, that usually feels a far cry from boundless love for all beings, but it is a start. It can help to keep us in contact with the reality that we are not entirely separate individuals.

When a tsunami hit Sri Lanka in December 2004, I had an insight into the depth and strength of this parent-child bond. We were on holiday there at the time, and I was sitting on our balcony in a small hotel on the south coast with my children and my partner, when we saw the sea suddenly come in and cover the short space between the beach and the road and, with three or four massive belches, reach the ground floor of our hotel. Broken by the coral reef around the bay, it was less of a wave and more like a gigantic bath that had suddenly overflowed. The force was incredible. Several metres high, the swirling brown water lifted cars, filled the houses, and crashed through the corrugated iron roofs below us. Planks of wood and other debris swirled around. We thought it would be only seconds before we, too, were engulfed by it. I felt trapped and terrified; we were already on the top floor and there was nowhere to go. For the first time in my life I really thought I was about to die.

Although my survival was threatened, there was no part of me that wanted to escape without my children; we were like a sealed unit. From the moment the tsunami hit and during the rumours of further waves and the frequent fear during the following two days, my mind was constantly

13

working on how to save Jai and Ella if the sea came back. Later, I listened to the reports of the scale of the disaster and the fact that so many of the dead were women and children. Many thousands of parents lost their lives trying to save their children. Later, we were relieved to meet a family we had got to know on the beach and hear that all four of their children had survived, though one had been hauled out of the sea three times by strangers. It was not only parents who risked their lives to save children, but this experience gave me an insight into the universality of my experience: that the parent-child bond is not just about me and mine but is felt by billions of people on this planet.

love as a threat to growth

As the tsunami reached the road, I saw a group of children watching it, petrified, for a split second and then pick up the ball they were playing with and run. I find it hard to im- agine they reached safety. People were screaming and I was aware of houses and people being covered by the sea right before our eyes. All I cared about at that moment was our survival; I wanted to save my family. I had no capacity to be open to the fate of others. In that moment, I felt I would willingly have sacrificed them all for my survival and that of my own children. I suspect I would have been capable of scrambling over the bodies of others to get us all to safety. Fortunately, I did not have to find out.

Yes, I saw the strength of the parent-child bond, but in retrospect I felt shocked and ashamed of shutting down to just me and mine so dramatically. With the help of a friend, I now see it as helpful to have had that insight into my own nature – into human nature – and to what it is to be human. And I saw the bottom line: I wanted to protect my children, but cherishing all beings was far from my experience when the chips were down and our lives were threatened. I saw clearly how the boundless heart may be our natural capacity to love, but there is a great deal that can get in the way; it certainly needs cultivation.

Simply experiencing love for our children is not sufficient to enable us to develop spiritually and cultivate a boundless heart. If it were, the human race would be in a very different situation, given the number of us who are parents. Worse, maybe there is even a danger that family life can be about extending our sense of a separate self to include one or more others, partner and children perhaps, huddling together behind strong defences, believing that we can hide, that we can defend ourselves against a seemingly hostile world in which everything changes. Our family could provide an illusion of security to protect us from the unpredictable flow of life, letting as little as possible in and as little as possible out. There is a danger that the very love we feel will lead us to close off to everything except me and mine, and hold tight to those we love, the way I held my children on the hillside above that Sri Lankan village once we had escaped from the hotel. In my mind, the image is of a shrinking down and away, curling up, cutting off from the world around us – the very opposite of growth.

Through listening to parents and reflecting on my own experience, I have come to see more clearly how the love we feel for our children is a precious gift and an opportunity for spiritual growth. It is an opening, a window. This can be a powerful kick-start to opening our heart more fully. It gives us an insight into our immense capacity to love, to cherish, and to care. Being a parent is a real opportunity to become aware of the depth and joy of the boundless heart, the unconditional love of which we are all capable. I find this a mind-blowing thought. I also find it deeply inspiring. It offers a glimpse of a vision that is far from the reality of how I feel and act most of the time, a vision of how I could be if I were to realize this potential.

reflecting on love

You, too, may perceive an ocean of difference between loving your children and meeting everyone in your life with that love, and you might ask how we can start to move from one to the other. One mother I met had spent a great deal of time reflecting on life within a close-knit family, concerned that this would cut her off from the wider world. She expressed the inherent opportunity in loving our children very eloquently when she said, 'Maybe any close relationship can be used either as a place to hide or a practice ground for engaging more deeply, more undefended, with what appears to be outside. Maybe what we are seeking is a deep, open, intimate, and mutually supportive relationship with every aspect of life. Maybe we could start with moving towards one other being in this way.'

We do not avoid the negative consequences of love for our children through not having children, or by holding ourselves back from wholeheartedly loving them – even if we could. It is better to relish and enjoy the glimpses of our boundless heart, love with all our heart, and do so within the context of a spiritual path and aspiring to live with our hearts open to life. We are all capable of feeling the love that makes us want to save other beings. As parents, it is often through our children that we know we are capable of that love. We can experience it. What I am interested in exploring is how to value feelings of parental love as an insight into our capacity to love and connect with other beings, and use it as a basis to allow our feelings of love to permeate our being, nourish us deeply, and extend that love to others.

The parent-child bond has the potential to teach us just what we are capable of when it comes to love. If I were truly in touch with a boundless heart, I would feel that bond with all sentient beings and I would not save myself or my children before any of them. I met a mother of two young boys who had spent time reflecting on the teachings embodied in the *Metta Sutta*. She realized that her love for her sons was the love she aspired to feel towards all beings. It was as if they had made a pact and she was their protector, but she held dear the aspiration to feel that same strength of love towards everything that lives on earth. Being a mother and having this bond with two other people helped to give her insight into what that bond could really mean.

I find it comforting to reflect that, according to the Buddha, sustaining a boundless loving heart, even for a moment, makes one a truly spiritual being. It is no small aspiration. For my part, I know the bottom line. I saw that in Sri Lanka. Opening out from loving one's own to loving more widely is a journey. It is unlikely to happen overnight. Along the way, there may be blissful flashes, or longer periods in which the love in our hearts naturally spreads wider and wider and we feel steeped in the desire for the well-being of everyone. Put more simply, the journey is about becoming a bit kinder every day.

I have found meditation very helpful within this journey. Meditation was what first drew me to Buddhism, but after a few years I started to question why I was spending my time doing this seemingly rather insular activity. And then I realized, prompted I am sure by something someone said. I meditate in order to become a little bit kinder every day. Since then, I have never questioned its value. Meditation is also about developing wisdom, perspective, and calm, but it is this desire to grow a little kinder every day that often sustains my motivation.

I notice progress, not so much by radiating waves of love all about me, as by reacting less to things that might have irritated me, or feeling genuinely pleased at a friend's success or good news, when previously my enthusiasm might have been curbed by feelings of envy or inadequacy. I may

simply find that I fly off the handle less easily when pro-
voked by one of my children, or be less inclined to mentally
beat myself up when I realize I have flown off the handle.
Or I might find myself better able to listen to a distressing
news report, and respond with compassion rather than
turning away. You might recognize some of these shifts in
yourself. We cannot feel compassion without love; compassion is the response that arises naturally when a loving
heart meets pain or suffering. All the great spiritual qualities we hear about – compassion, wisdom, equanimity –
boil down to how we express love and kindness day by
day, towards ourselves, our children, and others. The Dalai
Lama has said, 'My religion is kindness.' What would be
the point of spiritual progress and insight if I cannot be
kinder day by day and in the context of raising children?

a meditation on love

For me, to let the love that a mother feels for 'her child, her
only child' flow within all my relationships is a lofty but
galvanizing ideal. I find it amazing simply to realize that
aspiration is there, and most of us do have it. The reality is
that it is not easy to do, yet we can benefit from making that
intention conscious, reflecting on our potential to love and
our aspiration to love beyond me and mine, however small
our steps as we put that into practice. Buddhism has a great
deal to say about how to do this, and offers many teachings
on the subject of love and kindness, or loving-kindness
('*metta*', in the ancient Pali language). This includes a meditation handed down for more than 2,000 years, called the
metta bhavana. Bhavana means development or bringing
into being. This is a traditional Buddhist meditation to help
us fan the spark of loving-kindness and encourage it to
light and spread, starting with ourselves.

Below is a version of the metta bhavana that I have written
as a reflection or meditation to help us tune in to and build
on our feelings of love, however tentative or elusive they

may at first appear. The metta bhavana is traditionally divided into five stages, the first four focused on different people, spreading out in widening circles and – importantly – starting with ourselves. This well-wishing towards ourselves can feel counter-cultural for those of us in the West, but it is not really possible to love others unless we can love ourselves.

Try this meditation for yourself. If possible, sit quietly, in which case it usually helps to sit in an upright, dignified posture, and be comfortable and stable. Alternatively, you could try it while watching your children play, taking in any other children and adults around you, or anywhere you have a few spare minutes not talking to someone else. Or you might wish to do just two or three of the stages at suitable times during the day.

Throughout the meditation, you are not trying to force anything; simply dwelling with the intention and with whatever feelings are present is enough. If you resonate with the section from the *Metta Sutta* quoted above, you could try reading that. You can also consciously follow your breath in and out as a way to come into yourself and contact your feelings, and use short phrases to help, such as, 'May I be happy,' 'May they be happy.' I try to connect with the love I feel for my children and imaginatively embrace others with this love. Most important of all, accept that your mind will wander – that is just what minds do – and bring it gently back to the meditation or reflection as soon as you notice.

metta bhavana for parents

First, focus your attention on yourself as a parent, and connect with your love for your children. Let any feelings that arise be there naturally in your heart area. You may find you can wallow in and enjoy them, or you may feel anxious or tight, or you might feel nothing much. Whatever arises, be kind to yourself. You can try using imagination or memory to connect with love, maybe remembering a time when you did feel love. Marvel at your capacity to love, a window onto the boundless heart that is everyone's true nature, allowing it to gently build confidence in your potential to be a loving human being.

After a few minutes, picture a friend or family member who is also a parent. You may have seen signs of their love for their children, but whether you have or not, you can be confident of the bond they feel and that they deeply desire their children's health and happiness. Wish that for them too. Whether you are able to let go and enjoy basking in this warmth and well-wishing, or struggle to feel anything, it is the intention that is important.

Next, take your attention to someone you know less well, such as a neighbour or someone else you see regularly but have never got to know. As I write, I have in my mind someone I pass every morning as I take my daughter to school. She has three small girls, invariably dressed in pink. I have watched them progress from double buggy with toddler to all three running on ahead. She usually looks deeply harassed, head and attention forward. At other times she will smile in response to the charming way one of the girls greets me or to whatever they pass on their trip. Although it is not immediately evident, I can imaginatively engage with her love for her children and wish her well.

Next, bring to mind someone towards whom you may have difficult feelings, perhaps in relation to their parenting. Throughout this meditation, it helps to focus on what unites us all as human beings. Like you, this person ultimately wants to be happy and feel connected, and wants the same for their children. There is no need to get caught up in analysing why they behave in ways that are unlikely to lead to happiness. Perhaps they feel unable to cope. You will probably never know. Nor are you expecting to embrace them physically the next time you meet. You are simply extending love in widening circles and imaginatively directing well-wishing in their direction.

Finally, you can widen the circle still further to imaginatively sit with the people from each stage, maybe together watching your children playing happily in a beautiful setting, extending the feeling of kindness to include parents nearby and far away. You can experiment and be creative. You might include new parents, bowled over by their intensity of love and desire to protect as they hold their newborn babies, or new parents floundering in the uncertainty of how to be a parent, fearing failure or inadequacy. Indeed, these may be one and the same person at different times of the same day, or even the same hour. You can include parents skilfully finding ways to engage their teenagers in communication as they grow up, and parents who feel helpless or frustrated, ineffectually reacting like the teenagers themselves, or hitting out. You might bring to mind parents relishing giving presents to their children and enjoying their happiness, as well as those unable to feed their children.

However it is experienced and expressed, we all want to be happy, and we all want our children to be happy, to be at ease, to be nourished, safe, free from pain and emotional turmoil. You can imaginatively widen the circle to embrace them all, and you need not stop at parents or even people, but extend it to all forms of life with whom we share this earth.

letting go
Buddhism teaches us that we cannot be happy if we try to hold on to anyone or anything as fixed and unchanging, or as belonging to us. It is simply counter to the way things really are. Ultimately, everything changes and we lose everything, at the moment of death if not before. There is no solid ground, nothing outside ourselves that we can hold on to in order to feel permanently safe and secure.

That is the reality. In itself, this need not be a problem; it is our not seeing or refusing to accept it that leads to dissatisfaction, frustration, and unhappiness. It is in our constant trying to find happiness and security in other people and things that we keep hitting up against that reality. We lose people, precious moments in time, and cherished possessions, and it hurts.

These words may be very familiar to you. This is a fundamental teaching of Buddhism, and it also appears in many other religious and spiritual traditions. The teaching is certainly very familiar to me, yet I am aware there is a vast ocean of difference between hearing these words and actually living my life based on that understanding. I know it, but I rarely live it. There is an enormous gulf between knowing that no one will stay the same, and responding to everyone and everything as changing and transient. Yes, I can embrace them and love them with all my heart, but not cling to them.

Crossing that ocean is an integral part of spiritual development, at least from a Buddhist point of view. To do this, we need to feel, over and over again, how it feels to love and let go, and how it feels to love and try to hold fast. Then to notice the difference and reflect on it. We need to live that reality with awareness, innumerable times. It is a teaching we need to understand through our own experience. Feeling the difference can take us so much further than words. Through felt experience, we can really understand the teaching, and our responses gradually shift.

One of the things that emerged with crystal clarity as I researched this book was the extent to which being a parent offers such a wealth of opportunity to live this reality over and over again, and to open ourselves to loving and letting go. You must know as well as I do about the impossibility of holding on to your children at any particular stage. You may long for some particularly tricky phases to pass, but even in their passing there may be sadness and, at least from time to time, a reluctance to let go of those stages. For myself, the crinkly new baby phase disappeared too fast, leaving me longing to continue having babies. A friend was recently extolling the gorgeousness of the two-year-old phase, and her pain at the prospect of that passing all too soon, while her work took her away from her children more than she would have liked.

One day, I wrote the following about struggling with letting go the different stages, just one of many opportunities to experience love and letting go intertwined.

cleaning out the toy cupboard

Periodically, Ella and I tackle the toy cupboard. We make piles of what she and her brother have grown out of, and take them to the charity shop, relegate them to the bin, or pass the more treasured items to Sue's beloved daughter. It is a process we enjoy; harmonious team-work spiced with nostalgia, rolled up with the satisfactory outcomes of clear space, a job well done, and some forgotten games rescued with which we happily occupy a few hours.

One morning I went through that process alone, spurred by the need to take some toys to a family activity at the Buddhist centre the following day. Without the imperative of encouraging Ella to let go of her toys, I instead found myself lingering over some of them, wanting to keep them a little longer in case one or both of my children were to again experience the joy of building a brightly-coloured house and garden from Duplo blocks, remembering my delight at witnessing their cooperative and creative play, and my satisfaction that all was as it should be. It was easier to drop a couple of macho robots into the bag, the contrast highlighting my own expectations of how children should play. I kept the pirates and their ship, in the unlikely event that Jai would want them once more for a battle in the bath. Or was it me who wasn't ready to let them go? I smiled at Ella's individuality as I added the books about princesses and unicorns with which she had never resonated, always having preferred tales of adventurous girls and animals she can recognize as real.

More than anything, this process epitomizes letting go of each stage of my children's lives, and that morning brought home to me the resistance I feel within that, even though I generally pride myself in being rather good at it. True, I have felt shocked at having to buy Jai shoes larger than my own, but I have also appreciated being able to play badminton against him without being too careful how I return the shuttlecock. But with each clearing-out of the toy cupboard, I am forced to face the passing of yet another phase of what enthralled them and kept them happy for hours, days, or weeks at a time. Somehow, the baby toys were easier to let go, but now I am facing the fact that Jai is growing out of creative play and childhood. Unlike most of his friends, he has not left that behind completely, and he can still enter a world of vivid imagination from time to time. But soon there will hardly be a toy cupboard to clear any more, and it will contain games that even I find challenging, rather than simple train sets and Lego. In my heart I feel a mixture of sadness, excitement, delight, and pride as I watch them grow into themselves. But it is the sadness that is most present as I decide that I will, after all, take that big box of Duplo to the Buddhist centre.

By the time this book was nearing publication, I came face to face with the fact that there may be only a few more years of family holidays, playing with my children, and trying new things with them. But I don't want my life now to be dominated by the pain of that prospect. I want to enjoy them while they are here. I am aware that there is a wider teaching in my striving to do just that. From a Buddhist perspective, to love fully and consciously, to allow ourselves to feel that resistance to letting go while trying to embrace it and gradually accept the inevitability of change, is a strong spiritual practice in itself and has relevance far beyond our response to our children as they grow. If we let it, it can help erode some of the other habitual ways we respond to the world, gradually enabling us to live more in harmony with the way things are.

You can use imagination and reflection to experiment with how it feels to love with an awareness of the flow of change, and letting go into that, compared with holding on. You might bring to mind a memory of loss, or try to be fully conscious of the process of change, as I did when sorting through the toys. In fact, clearing out books and toys can be a good opportunity. There are big events too, like a new school, a first sleepover, or making a journey on their own. There are also the smaller changes: I was stopped in my tracks when my son asked for pyjamas 'without pictures on' – a sign of growing up I was completely unprepared for.

A good way to explore the experience is to develop curiosity towards your thoughts and feelings. What is going on? Is there a sense of panic? A desire to snatch back? Excitement and anticipation? A delight in the new replacing the old? Sadness? Happiness? A mixture? Or very little to feel at all?

There is no right answer to those questions. Try just to be aware of your thoughts and feelings. Then try to engage with a desire to hold on and protect, to hold close, not wanting to let go, wanting it to last just a little longer. How does that feel in the area around your heart? Or notice the thoughts in your head. Then imaginatively open your hands and heart to let your children grow and be who they are and move away from you in that moment. I find the image of opening my hands powerful and evocative. You may want to play with different ways to get some sense of felt experience of the difference between the two responses.

Opportunities to do this constantly present themselves. We can become more aware that when we want to hold on to someone, we risk something closing down inside. I feel it as a restriction or tightness and sadness, even as I engage with it to write this chapter. When we let go, we feel bigger. Maybe we still feel sad, at least for a while, but I can certainly feel something release in me when I imaginatively open my hands and let go.

Separation and letting go is a constant thread, from well before the first day at nursery to far beyond the day a child leaves home. Parenting is an opportunity to reflect on the pain that comes with not wanting to let go. All we can really do is acknowledge it, let it be there, be aware how it feels, and reflect on it. We also recall how we hold this awareness in the context of the spiritual path, however that may manifest. With such an awareness, and within that context, our responses do gradually shift, enabling us to meet more experiences with open hands and heart. Being aware of loving and letting go will enable us to love more wholeheartedly, both within the family and way beyond. For me, it is not just about embracing new phases of my children's lives, or enabling me to be a better parent; it is about how staying open to change can lead to an openness to life. These changes embrace the ebb and flow of relationships, of work partnerships, of parents getting older, even the reality of climate change. Closing down does not help in any of those situations either. The only answer is openness to the reality of change, whether we like it or not.

letting our children be who they are

I remember Ella's beady eyes as a newborn child, seemingly so wise and aware. I remember gazing at this being and wondering where she, already so knowing, could have come from. This set me questioning why are we here and where any of us come from. Children are themselves; they are more than the sum of the parts contributed by their parents. Seeing our children arrive, as beings in their own right, can provide food for reflection, and thoughts can arise about rebirth, the fact that we don't own our children, and the need to let our children be who they are. For all our investment, love, and involvement, we can also be curious about our children and who they are. We may have assumptions about our children, and we can influence them, but can we really know them? A mother of two young adults spoke to me about watching her daughters' lives starting to unfold, reflecting on what her children had brought into this life, knowing how complex people are, and giving them space to be who they were and explore themselves.

Letting go forces us to confront our fears, not just of losing our children completely (or their losing us), but losing them in small ways. It is not only the big moves, such as the start of school or leaving home. It happens each time they choose a different opinion to mine, dream of a career I disapprove of, or behave in ways I would prefer they didn't. That is a daily, if not constant, process. Wanting to hold on can manifest as a reluctance to let our children be who they are, as opposed to who we would like them to be.

One mother talked in particular about going through this chain of thoughts, fears, and desires, over and over again. She would experience the fear of her daughters stepping away from her and want to hold them back, knowing that she loved them and wanted the best for them. Life went on. Things changed. She did her best. Then she would get stuck again. She described how she felt this fear over and over again. She saw it as part of the ongoing reflection on what human life is about.

> *I have experienced the relationship with my children as taking step after step backwards, until one day I hope I will see these unique beings that are in some ways just as separate from me, or part of me, as any unique beings, so that I can appreciate them for who they are, not what I want them to be. I have a long way to go.*

Here, too, is a teaching and experience that we can allow to permeate our lives inside and outside the family. We can learn to respond not just to our children in that way but to more and more people, in ever-widening circles. It can help counteract the tendency to want our partner or work colleagues to behave in certain ways, to be different, or to be their lovely selves minus a couple of irritating traits. And then it can flow far wider than that and manifest as greater patience, tolerance, and acceptance. Just as experiencing our capacity to love can give us insight into our boundless heart, remaining aware and keeping our hands open as our children grow can enable us to live more in harmony with the way things are, within and beyond our family.

2

give and take

The Buddhist texts contain rich tales of people striving for spiritual attainment in ideal situations, far from the busy cities, sometimes in large gatherings, sometimes in solitude. One story tells of a follower of the Buddha who is meditating in a mango grove. For one friend of mine, the mango grove came to symbolize all she craved and felt denied as a mother of three and deputy head of a large school: beauty, tranquillity, silence, time to sit and reflect. Instead, she felt her life was a constant round of responding to people's needs and problems.

So how do we follow a spiritual path in the midst of the demands on us as parents? Is it even possible without a mango grove in which to sit? Are there ways to create our own version of the mango grove, however briefly?

giving and generosity

Generosity is, according to Buddhism, the first of the qualities of Enlightenment.[2] The Buddha himself always started by teaching newcomers about *dana*, the practice of mutual generosity, and said that no spiritual life is possible without a generous heart. One quote from the Buddha that I find particularly powerful and pertinent in this context is,

> *If you knew, as I do, the power of giving,*
> *you would not let a single meal pass*
> *without sharing some of it.*[3]

This is good news for parents. It is one area in which we may have a head start when it comes to spiritual growth. The spaciousness and tranquillity of the mango grove might seem to belong on another planet, our minds may be full of practicalities and our patience may be tested, but giving comes with the territory. You probably don't let many meals pass without sharing them. Thoughts about how to juggle childcare with work, what to cook, past conversations, future obligations, and frustrations over a lack of time, may feel anything but spacious. But giving is inbuilt, a daily ritual not dependent on generous urges. We have to give so much as parents, often going beyond what we feel capable of, because the situation demands it. And we certainly need to share our meals.

You can probably get a sense why generosity is so fundamental by remembering a time when you did act with generosity, and exploring what it felt like. Or bring to mind someone you think of as generous and notice how you feel about them. Generosity is beautiful and powerful because it opens us to the liberating qualities of letting go and a joyous sense of freedom. Generosity also counteracts our natural tendency to hold on to what we want, while pushing away what we don't want. Within this context, we can come to see giving as a gift in itself, rather than a distraction from things spiritual. As parents, we have so many opportunities to use generosity to transform daily acts of giving into spiritual practice.

Mothers start giving to their children as soon as they are conceived, spontaneously and naturally providing them with nutrients through the umbilical cord. Almost as soon as her umbilical cord was cut, I put Ella to the breast, thinking she might be hungry after eighteen hours of labour. I was lucky. I glowed with health during pregnancy. I loved feeling the growing baby in my womb, and usually enjoyed breast-feeding. I found it magical that my body produced all my babies needed in their first few months of life, and did so responsively. It was also a time when I could stop and sit and do very little except feed the baby – at least with Jai. After Ella arrived, I would frequently have to wrench her from the breast and dump her unceremoniously on the sofa or floor to respond to a toddler crisis. However, even with Ella, I had intimate times of feeding her in peace, gazing into each other's eyes, holding her tiny fingers, feeling complete, happy, and wanting to give all I could, all that was needed.

As my children grew, feeding time became a considerably less satisfying experience. Producing healthy food that they were willing to eat felt repetitive and not at all creative, and then there was the struggle to keep them at the table for longer than a few minutes before being left to face the washing-up. I often felt the same about the bedtime routine. From supper to sleep could take three hours and leave me feeling drained and tearful with exhaustion. This did not feel anything like generosity, but a grinding, continual response to their needs, fulfilling my obligations as their mother.

So what is the difference? Reflecting on my experience of feeding children helps me clearly see that what marks the distinction between resentment and generosity is not the experience itself – some people feel trapped by breastfeeding and enjoy cooking – but in *how* we give. Giving and generosity are not the same thing. *How* we give is of paramount importance. As parents, our spiritual life in unlikely to include profound experiences in mango groves or other such peaceful oases. Instead, we have many rich opportunities to bring our spiritual aspirations to our daily interactions with our children and others, particularly when it comes to giving. In this way, we transform giving into generosity. For me, this means pausing and catching myself feeling resentful about producing supper, again, and trying to bring in that intention – however tentative my connection with it – to practise being generous.

growing as a parent through giving

One inspiring example of how we can transform giving into generosity, and thereby our experience of how we give, was described by one Buddhist mother who consciously set out to transform a number of household tasks. Ironing was one of them. It was something she didn't enjoy but needed to do regularly. Choosing to continue to do the family ironing herself, she decided it was not good enough to do it with subtle feelings of irritation, and set out to transform it into a practice of love and generosity. Over the next three weeks, the piles of ironing continued to accumulate, but she completely transformed her experience of doing the ironing.

transforming ironing

Rather than be resistant and fed up with ironing for other people, I saw it as an expression of my care for them. I carefully set up my posture, making sure I felt comfortable, and with my back straight I brought to mind the person for whom I was ironing. I found that my state of mind became expanded, rather than contracted, by reflecting on love or on a clear blue sky. What I found encouraging was that I didn't have to do this consciously for very long before it became a permanent shift. My attitude towards ironing shifted, and that gave me the faith that I could turn round other aspects of my life also. I have since had that experience. It is possible to change things fundamentally within only two or three weeks if we only bring awareness to them.

Another Buddhist mother of two told me she sometimes imagines herself in a Buddhist nunnery, cooking for the nuns, and that there is no real difference. She would still cook every day if she worked in a nunnery. It's the background commitment that is important. Everything gets filtered through that commitment. It's about trying to make everything align with that commitment. Another mother told me how she approached cooking for her family.

transforming cooking

Cooking is something I enjoy, and that is important in terms of the family. I cook, and then we all sit down to eat together. For this reason, I created a shrine box for my vegetable knife. It is a shrine to Amitabha, the Buddha of infinite light, with a slot for the knife. It helps me connect with awareness and loving-kindness every time I pick up the knife. Cooking with loving-kindness is transformative. Cooking with irritation and anger is not a satisfactory experience.

The cause of irritation, impatience, or frustration lies not in the total dependence of the baby on its mother's milk, or the hours of bedtime routine. Nor is it the need to coax reluctant children through each step towards bed and the end of another day. The cause of both my 'suffering' and my joy when feeding my children was how I responded to giving them what they needed day by day. One of my favourite Buddhist teachings – the teaching of the two arrows – relates to this. It is relevant in transforming how we give, and also in bringing awareness to our response to things.

The Buddha suggested that two 'arrows' hit us every time something happens to us.[4] The first is the event itself, the second is how we react to it. You can probably come up with examples of how this happens for you. One example for me would be walking into the kitchen to cook, feeling tired and wishing someone else was there to produce a delicious meal and look after me. That is a very real situation, and not especially easy. But on top of this I could unconsciously pile secondary arrows, along the lines of, 'It's always the same,' 'This is never-ending,' 'I'll never have enough sleep,' 'No one cares for me,' 'I can't cope.' These arrows pile on the pain, making the situation much worse and taking me even further from my simple desire that my children and I are well fed and happy, from confidence that I can do what is necessary, and from the possibility of a more creative response, such as cooking what I like for once instead of what my children like.

We can learn a great deal from trying to separate the two arrows. We need to look back and separate the event (such as a child refusing to go to sleep) from our reaction to it. Try it for yourself, becoming aware what is going through your mind when you feel overwhelmed by demands or resentful about giving. Try to work out what the first arrow is and which thoughts or emotions come about by your shooting the second arrow. You might also notice your own expectations and assumptions (for example, 'This child *should* sleep.') and how they affect your thoughts and feelings of injustice, anger, or exasperation.

It need not be that way. We can learn to respond differently. It takes time and practice, often conscious practice, but we can all do it, and through that grow wiser and kinder every day. I sometimes still feel the same as I go into the kitchen to think about supper, but more often than not I don't, and I now quite often enjoy cooking, as I did before I had children. That might not seem immediately important as spiritual progress, but I can view such shifts from the perspective of wanting to meet all of life with engagement and generosity, not resistance and resentment. It also makes my life – and that of my children – considerably more pleasant.

I have also found that bringing to mind the fact that nothing lasts for ever, especially when it comes to children, is helpful in shifting *how* I react to the daily acts of giving inherent in parenting. For example, I gradually realized that I had very little time left when my son wanted me to climb into his bed and cuddle him before he slept. I am glad I could appreciate that phase before it passed completely.

Sometimes I used to lie with Ella as she fell asleep, and as I gently extracted my arm she would clasp it the moment her slumbering body sensed the movement, often with great force. Sometimes that made us both giggle, but at times when I had hoped for a quick getaway, my mind already busy with what I was going to do next, I felt irritated. At those times, I tried to pause and remind myself that her wanting me like that would not last, and there was no more precious way to spend the five extra minutes she was pleading for (she falls asleep quickly) than to hold her and watch her face as she fell asleep. During the time it took to write this book, that phase had mostly passed too.

giving the gift of fearlessness

When I declined my son's challenge to jump from the top diving board at the pool, I sealed my daughter's fate, at least for the time being. If she knew I was scared, she had little hope of facing the same thing herself.

You don't need to reflect much to realize how much fear you hold, and you can probably think of times when fear has prevented you from doing something. Fear can take many forms. Most forms of fear we experience occur at a lower level and less pronounced than the heart-pounding fear that makes itself known when we watch horror films or enter the unknown. For example, anxiety may be more common, whether it is about the future, about our own performance, or fear of being judged if our children don't behave as they should. It might be fear of how they will behave at table with their grandparents, whether they will share things when they go to nursery, or receive good reports – anything. Within parenting, the opportunities to feel such anxieties are endless.

Almost always, anxiety or fear pertains to something other than the present moment. Try listing some fears that occupy your mind. On my list would be fear that my children will be involved in an accident, that they will be rejected or lonely at school, or that they will get into drugs. Although I am enjoying writing this, every so often another fear creeps in – that I am not good enough or not enough of an expert to write – and then my mind goes foggy and I lose touch with the desire simply to offer what I can. Sometimes I become aware of a free-floating anxiety: when one anxiety is removed, I instantly become anxious about something else. Go through the fears you have listed. How many are about something happening right now? The tsunami excepted, I am rarely frightened by objective danger here and now, yet fear does affect my life and close me down, and this is counter to the more open response to life that I aspire to.

Although I refused the diving board, I did happily embrace the opportunity to jump off a cliff high above the Dordogne River on a family holiday some time later. I went first, followed by my son and my partner. We each ran to the edge and were pulled up into the sky. My heart was pounding, but my fear turned to laughter with sheer joy at the experience of my first paragliding flight. However, as my then nine-year-old daughter was later swept past me, strapped to the instructor I had met only a couple of hours earlier, my heart lurched as if to leave my body. I gasped, blood rushing to my face and tears to my eyes, the words 'my baby' on my lips. I had persuaded them to take her up, even though they were somewhat reluctant because she was so light, and then spent an anxious half hour waiting for her to be safely delivered with no bones broken and flushed with the exhilaration of the flight. She had watched me go and, as far as I could tell, fear did not even occur to her. I am very glad of that.

What could be more empowering the gift of fearlessness? The gift of fearlessness is possibly the greatest gift I can give to my children. If we bring our children up with fearlessness, we cultivate their ability to make their own choices and think for themselves, and not be afraid to be different, not go along with something they don't agree with just so that they can blend in with their school friends. Fearlessness is not a lack of awareness of danger or fool-hardiness. I spent two years travelling alone in Latin America, and people described me as brave, but I was more naive than fearless, and I was pretty safe, at least most of the time. Fearlessness is an ability to be aware of the conse-quences and to make choices: to feel the fear and do it any-way, as the famous book title suggests.

Within the gift of fearlessness lie encouragement, inspir-ation, and self-confidence, yet we cannot wrap these up or put them on the table like meals. Like any positive quality, fearlessness and self-confidence are not so much handed over as sparked off in others by how we ourselves behave. We have to live it to give it. We cannot raise children with a positive and open attitude to life if our own is fearful and closed, if we are wary of the unknown. Giving the gift of fearlessness calls us to be our biggest selves – to embrace the unknown, to embrace fear, and live our lives to the full.

The summer after our paragliding adventure, we tried white-water kayaking. I loved this too, but I found it quite difficult and, at times, frightening to be in a kayak with Ella, having to give such instructions as 'paddle hard on the left now!' trying desperately not to let my voice betray my rising panic. At one point, we were told to do what we should do if we fell out of the kayak in white water, which was to lie on our backs looking up at the sky and allow the river to carry us to a calm place where we could swim to the side and get out. As I stretched out my hand to help Ella scramble over the rocks to get back into the river, I saw she was crying. I reassured her that she didn't have to do it if she didn't want to, but all she did was shake her head, unable to speak but refusing to go back. In the end, I helped her into the river as far as I could and let go of her, watched her being carried quickly away from me, and then I got in too and lay back. Within minutes, Ella was delighting in talking about the experience with her brother and cousins, and when we got home and were all doing a quick-fire recount of the holiday to my partner, Ella proudly reported, 'And I faced my fear!' I still feel proud of my previously rather physically timid daughter.

Ella did feel fear, lots of it, but she chose not to be governed by it, not to let it stop her taking part in an experience she wanted to share with the rest of us. Similarly, I fear losing my children, as do all parents. It shouldn't come as a surprise to me when it manifests in different anxieties and fears along the way. I also know that I have a choice in how I respond to that feeling, and that how I respond will have an effect, maybe an immediate effect, on both me and my children. In the longer term, fear threatens to make me less open to life, less able to speak out about what is important, and risk others catching it: fear is contagious. Of course, fear can be a warning that something is, in fact, dangerous. But this is far from always being the case.

Part of the process involved in giving the gift of fearlessness is simply being aware that the fear is there and seeing it for what it is. We don't have to not feel it or get rid of it. If we can turn towards our experience and recognize it for what it is, this gives us an important breathing space in which we can then make a choice about responding. You might find it helpful to label it, 'Oh, here is fear,' letting it be there without pushing it away or letting it take over. Curiosity can be very useful too. See if you can find a way to be curious about this fear. What is the feeling in your heart, throat, or other part of your body? Examine it in some detail, exploring whether it feels tight, or hot or cold, for example. In the same way, try to notice the thoughts going through your mind. There is no need to get caught by the storylines. Just see if you can notice them and maybe list them. Rather than pushing away or closing off to the feeling of fear, open to it, turn to it, and look at it with curiosity. You might even find you wonder at some of the storylines and how insubstantial they really are. It can even be quite an amusing process.

This is easier said than done. Like bringing awareness to any aspect of our experience, it takes practice. The more we can learn to bring our awareness to our thoughts, feelings, and emotions under more favourable conditions, the more it is possible to bring our awareness to strong emotions such as fear as well. It is possible, and having a choice about how to respond is wonderful – a real freedom – so it is worth it! This freedom, when I am in touch with it, helps me make better choices and access the gifts of confidence and fearlessness I want to pass on to my children and to others. While I do what I can to keep us safe as a family, I don't want fear to govern how we live and prevent us all from embracing opportunities for new and wonderful experiences, or for living life to the full, just as I didn't want it to stop any of us getting as close as we probably ever will to flying like a bird.

going beyond ourselves by giving

I remember repeatedly getting up during the night to tend to my children when they were little, or when they were ill, sometimes exhausted or ill myself. It felt almost impossible to drag myself from the depths of sleep yet again. Sometimes I lost my sense of time and perspective, sometimes I felt desperation or violent rage at the intrusion into my sleep. Yet I had to drag myself into the room next door and do what was necessary to settle and quieten them. I rarely felt generosity or boundless love at such moments. I sometimes wept with exhaustion and frustration. It was all I could do simply to do what was necessary without violence or unkindness. That had to be enough, and I believe it was enough.

This is a common enough experience when parenting babies and young children. Unfortunately, such night-time demands do not, in themselves, lead to growth in wisdom and kindness. Yet going beyond ourselves in response to our children also indicates what we are capable of: giving so much more than we think we can. This can become a path to growth when we choose to reflect on it in quieter moments – or when lying in bed and unable to get back to sleep after the latest interruption.

Recognizing what you have managed to do may help give you confidence in yourself and your capabilities. Reflecting on where you accessed the resources to respond – once again – may also offer a glimpse of what is bigger than us in the universe, of the love and positive energy that flows all the time and can nourish and support us when we choose to lean into it or go beyond ourselves. Perhaps we are not limited by our personal energy store. You may also want to reflect on the potential within that. If you are capable of going beyond yourself to give to that extent with your children, how would life be if you were more able to be open in every aspect of your life, without feeling so depleted? That might seem inconceivable, but that is what we would do if we were Enlightened. Going beyond ourselves to reach out to one or two other beings is a start.

According to Buddhism, as we grow wiser, we dissolve the sense of ourselves as separate from other people, feeling and responding from the basis of our connectedness. That is another distant and lofty concept, but raising children can help soften the boundaries between ourselves and other people and loosen our view of our personal limitations. Softening and loosening in this way releases the space to breathe and to grow, even if it does feel intensely uncomfortable at times, and anything other than 'spiritual'.

One father I spoke to said that his main spiritual practice while raising two small boys was attempting true tolerance in the face of an existence without real personal boundaries, and that this had done more to help him surrender personal preferences – and loosen up who he was and who he could be – than many years of what might traditionally have been seen as more spiritual living situations. It is much harder to stay separate and hold on to our individual likes and dislikes when we so frequently have to let go of our immediate needs and desires to see to those of someone else, especially babies and very young children.

yet we also need time out

By the end of an extended family holiday, on which I took no time out at all, I found it hard to answer the question, 'How are you?' If the children were happy, I was fine; if they were dissatisfied and complaining, it had a disproportionate effect on me and coloured how I was too. My well-being was vulnerable to how someone else was behaving. Losing touch with ourselves in this way means our happiness is constantly under threat, because someone else holds in their tiny hands control for how we are. Personally, I soon find that makes it harder for me to bring awareness to my experience or respond with openness or creativity.

A friend recently quoted to me, 'Having children is like having your heart wrenched out and walking around outside yourself.' I instantly saw what she meant. Particularly when children are young and you spend a lot of time with them, not having them there can feel as though you are missing a limb. We therefore need to be able to come back to ourselves, to feel our heart is back in our chest, and to feel whole as an individual alone. Even though our lives and our loves are intimately entwined, we are not our children and they are not us. There are times when that reality gets lost. Perhaps we can also love even more fully if we can be whole, interconnected, and loving, yet see our children as whole too.

I believe in time out from the family. I am convinced of the benefits of quiet, preferably solitary, time away from one's children, whether in short snatches or for longer periods of time in the mango grove. This may sound like a contradictory statement in a book about the opportunity to blossom spiritually in the context of family life, but I firmly believe in both. I don't know how I would survive without it; I would certainly have been more difficult to live with, and found it harder to keep hold of the thread that connects me with my spiritual aspirations.

Taking time out feels to me like looking at my life through a camera lens and zooming out to take in more of the world that surrounds me, away from the narrow, close-up perspective when spending a lot of time with children. Children do tend to home in on things, and there is much that is wonderful to be learned from that, as I discuss later, but there are also innumerable benefits to being able to take a step back and look more calmly and objectively at our situation. Taking a couple of steps back can help us to see things from a different perspective. It can help us to sink down in our bodies and tap into how we feel, and the way we lead our lives, in the clear light of day.

This shift of perspective moves us into the open air, under a wide open sky, with a sense of space. Within this space, even if anxieties and crowds of thoughts still circulate in the mind, there is more room between them and me, and I identify less closely with them. A thought, feeling, or emotion may still demand my attention, but with the benefit of extra space, I can more often choose whether to look at it or not, and have confidence that it will pass, or certainly lose its power. From that calmer, more objective space, I can see my life more clearly, face what I don't like, and connect with how I want to be – again and again.

Time out for me usually includes the opportunity to go deeper with meditation. This I also find deeply nourishing and important. The opportunity for more consolidated practice of bringing awareness to myself and what I am doing makes a huge difference when I later do that back in the midst of family life. Finally, it is also necessary simply to rest. My view of myself and my children could be warped by exhaustion, especially when they were very young, giving me the incorrect impression that the current situation was never-ending.

time out in small chunks
Unlike Prince Siddhartha, who left his family to go forth on a spiritual quest and later became the Buddha, I don't believe we have to leave for very long. Substantial amounts of time alone can be precious and scarce for a parent. One trick is to learn some short-cuts that enable you to make the most of opportunities to create some space, take a quiet pause, and come back to yourself from time to time. Daily meditation has been a lifeline for me, nourishing me, bringing me back to myself, and grounding me, reminding me again and again that I am a being on a spiritual path. It is so easy to lose touch with this bigger picture that organizes the priorities in my life, and so important to find ways to remember.

You may have your own particular places or activities to bring you back to yourself, which help you to maintain a sense of sanity and perspective. This might be a weekly class, reading, using the time when walking to work, or a few hours of personal time set aside now and again. I find it is also possible to take time out while my children are physically present but temporarily self-sufficient or, when they were very tiny, asleep or peaceful in a buggy or backpack.

I used to visit a nearby piece of old woodland with my baby in a backpack, and later with my children and their friends when they were still biddable enough to join me and delight in climbing over fallen trees and kicking the leaves. While the children were safely absorbed, I would pause and look up at the sky through the branches, stroke the twists of hawthorn, or lean against an ancient tree. Since my children lost interest, I still find time to visit. I love the

43

hawthorn branches that make unexpected twists and turns as if continuously avoiding obstacles. I give my weight to the tree and use my imagination to engage with its age and wisdom, everything it has seen pass by, the depth of the roots, the solidity, the way it reaches towards the sky. This was a quick way to bring myself into the present, remind myself of the bigger context to my life: to live with an open heart and feel love, expansiveness, and happiness. Whatever is going on when I arrive in the woods seems somehow different by the time I leave, usually less than an hour later.

I admit, however, that despite the fact that I know what is good for me and do have such short-cuts, I rarely take them. I get caught up in the busyness and apparent urgency of what I am doing, jumping from one thing to another, although I know, deep down, that I need time out. Maybe that resonates with your experience. I think it is important to recognize that the weight of what we are doing can develop its own momentum. Sometimes the only option is just to do it – ignore the resistance and turn off the computer, put one's coat on, and go to the woods for some breathing space.

There is something powerful about taking my life out under an open sky to gain a wider perspective when I have little time available. Camping by the Dordogne River on a family holiday, I could understand how, according to Buddhist scriptures, people have become Enlightened by watching a river flowing past them. There was something powerful about a week of watching the flow of a river, the parties of people in canoes, and the water, flowing from the mountains towards the sea. The constant reminder that everything flows and changes had a deeply calming and nourishing effect on my body, mind, and heart and provided a broader perspective without the need for more than a few minutes at a time away from my children.

longer periods of time away

I have also benefited enormously from blocks of a day, a weekend, or a week or two away on a meditation or study retreat, where I can take stock and see myself and my life in a broader perspective, breathe more freely, let go of the need to organize others, and reconnect with the fact that I have spiritual aspirations and with how I want to live my life. Longer periods of time out also enable me to learn how it feels to be aware, and this has helped me to make use of windows of opportunity, and led me to clarify my priorities so that I can open such windows. In the four years between learning to meditate and having children, I went on retreats several times a year, but I felt a sense of mounting panic during my pregnancy. When would I be able to go on retreat again? How would I survive without that intensive bout of meditation?

I was able to leave each of my children for a while just after their first birthdays. When Jai was born, I was working in an international aid agency. I said I would not travel until he was at least a year old. I found myself on a flight to Peru a week after his first birthday. I left that job after Ella was born and booked a week's retreat some time ahead, allowing time for her to be weaned. I was really pleased and grateful that I had that retreat to look forward to, a light at the end of what sometimes seemed a long and exhausting tunnel of baby, toddler, and work.

As the retreat drew nearer, I became more and more anxious about leaving her. I had the same experience before leaving Jai to go to Peru. I willed almost anything to happen, any external intervention that might prevent me going. A broken leg would have done nicely. Leaving them was an enormous wrench, though on both occasions I left them in the capable arms of their father. It evoked an image of pulling apart a lump of dough, the two halves connected by ever thinner threads until they are so stretched they are forced to let go.

For the first few days of that retreat when I first left Ella, every time somebody walked into the room my heart jumped in fear. I was convinced they were coming to tell me about a dreaded phone call, accident, hospitalization, or even death of one or both of my children. Of course, they had completely different reasons for coming in, nothing to do with me. In between these incidents, I did appreciate the space. I felt waves of gratitude for the existence of that particular retreat centre, and the ease with which I could take refuge there and feel safe, spacious, and supported. But overall I was anxious. I called home every day, often feeling far from fully present on the retreat, and it was hard to bear my fear of bad news.

I still wonder why I put myself through it. I find it hard to believe that I went away at all, feeling as I did. But I went. There was something even stronger that took me on retreat, a conviction that was greater than my reluctance to leave. Looking back, I see that conviction as faith and a desire to grow. I wanted to live more fully, to be more alive, to be kinder, bigger, and happier. I knew, deep down, that it was important for me to take time out from my family to help me realize my potential, then bring what I had learned back into the family. It was a powerful force that somehow overrode my reluctance.

Towards the end of that one-week retreat, something shifted in me, though it was barely perceptible. I felt something twist round in my body, and I had a strong sense that although I still didn't know how I would ever recover from the grief and loss I feared, I would physically continue to live and have an existence if my children were to die before me. I had a visual image of myself as a being beyond and without them. Although considering their deaths is still unbearably painful, that momentary vision did have a strong effect on me, almost as if I too was being weaned and placed back on my own two feet, connecting with the reality that I was not exclusively the mother of my children. Somehow, that glimmer made me feel more whole, stronger, less vulnerable, and less anxious. I was no less bound up in my children, and certainly no less in love with them. If anything, I was more so. But it was a crucial glimpse into myself as an individual as well as a mother.

Longer chunks of time away have also enabled me to see how I am changing and growing. I have met other Buddhist parents who had not gone on retreat for a few years after their children were born, so they had assumed that they had not changed very much, at least in terms of their spiritual aspirations. However, when they did have time to stop and look at themselves, they were pleasantly surprised to see that they had changed and grown considerably. When I look back over my spiritual development, it seems like a series of steps, with the positive changes and the turning points nearly always happening when I am away on retreat. It was not so much that the changes only happened on retreat, but the time was an opportunity to take stock and go deeper.

finding a balance
We need to use our intuition to decide how often to go away and for how long. It's a matter of finding a balance. Sometimes I need to be firm, even if I appear hardhearted, and have the confidence of my convictions to leave for more than a day or two. One of the mothers I interviewed described how much she had needed the courage of her convictions every Tuesday night when she left for a class at the Buddhist centre, with her daughters clinging to her legs and crying, 'Don't leave me, Mummy!' But my whole family benefits from my taking time out, which has enabled me to follow through most of the decisions I have made over the years.

Of course, it is possible to go away too much, to see the spiritual life as being 'out there', or to shut ourselves away too firmly, too often, or for too long in order to study or meditate. It would be uncomfortable to be left with a nagging feeling that I took myself away too much, missed fleeting and enchanting moments of their childhood, or to hear in the future that they considered me to have been absent. There can be no general rule. I mainly manage my work around school hours, so I am around before and after school most days. I go out one, or rarely two, evenings a week and my children often choose to spend time with their friends. But they still sometimes complain that I am hardly ever there. For many years I found a reasonable compromise was to go on one residential retreat a year, for one or two weeks, plus a couple of weekends, and do all I could to lean against trees or meditate in the mean time. I avoided reading about what was on offer when I couldn't easily get away, in order to minimize feeling constrained.

Taking time out from your children may be difficult both practically and emotionally, particularly if you are a single parent, or have a partner who is unable to fill the gap. If there are limited weeks available for family holidays, one week alone may seem out of the question. However, it is a question worth asking. It is not always impossible to get away, and I believe it is worth seriously considering before dismissing the idea, even if you don't much *want* to go away, even for a day. Among those I meet at the school gate, I know I am in a small minority who chooses to go away on her own, for herself rather than a work obligation. I also firmly believe that my family have benefited greatly from my taking time out.

This is one reason why friends who understand and share our spiritual aspirations are important. Friends who are not parents can help challenge us if we believe it is impossible to get away. Maybe it really is impossible, but it may be worth stopping now, to think about it.

- If you don't want to go, why not?

- What are the implications of taking a day, a few days, or a week away from your family?

- What would have to be in place for you to be dispensable for a short while?

Conflict, guilt, and doubt are often associated with leaving children, on top of piecing together elaborate practical arrangements for a replacement. It can help to be aware that such emotions are likely to arise. I relived all three when I anticipated a retreat in Scotland, and I went round in circles. It was a very special retreat and a precious opportunity to spend time with the woman who ordained me, so I had booked it despite it being in term time. I looked forward to it for months, but as the time drew near, I was anxious and didn't want to go. How could I leave my children? Scotland was such a long way. It was madness to go away in the middle of the school term. I needed to be here, continuing to establish a workable homework routine with Jai. Ella protested whenever she had an evening without my putting her to bed. How would they survive without me? But it was too good an opportunity to miss. I would learn a lot, enjoy the space and the mountains, and I would come back energized, positive, and refreshed. They would miss me, but what was five days? They would get over it soon enough. Who was clinging to whom?

It is relatively easy for me to go on retreat during school holidays. In any case, Jai and Ella spend half of each school holiday with their father, so they leave me and are happy, and I feel free to go. But this level of conflict and doubt was still familiar territory from when they were very young. Anticipating a retreat months in advance, and actually leaving when it comes to it, are two different things. It has helped me to know that conflicting thoughts and emotions are bound to be present, and I remind myself that there is no absolute right or wrong decision. There will be positive and negative aspects whether I go or not. Once we see that, we can make a calmer decision. On that occasion, I drove myself and my partner mad, going round in circles for a week or two, then I cancelled my retreat booking. But more often, I have felt the resistance and gone away in spite of it, and I have never regretted that choice.

It can also be hard to come back, to rejoin a family that has been living a completely different experience and, possibly, go through a time of subconscious 'punishment' from small children and a very tired partner. In my experience, this difficult phase is very brief, and being aware that this might happen is helpful. I used to be in tears by the end of every retreat, and I would have to be peeled gently off the doorframe and loaded into a taxi to leave the safety of the retreat centre and go home to all that would assault me the minute I walked through the door. However, once the journey was over I would always be delighted to see my family again. After a while I got used to the transition. I find it helps to engage immediately with what has been going on for my children, see any punishment or resentment for what it is, and know that it will soon pass.

Seeing our daily lives in a longer-term perspective, as we do when we step back or step into the open air, we see that everything passes. Within that knowledge, we can also see the loveliness of the stages of parenting as they pass, and feel a renewed motivation to embrace those stages and enjoy our children as they grow. This perspective, in turn, brings us more fully present when we return to our children after time out. Time away can help us see our lives from a healthier perspective, experience ourselves as individuals as well as parents, and see how we have grown. It may even seem contradictory that a book celebrating the inherent opportunities to flourish spiritually within family life is simultaneously advocating time out, but I see untold benefits and retain the right to believe in both.

3

getting to know ourselves

I found myself seated in a small, tidy living room facing a
woman I admired very much. Nearly three decades of Buddhist practice shone through her. Slight and neat, centred
and wise, her very presence radiated calm. Against that
background, it was initially somewhat incongruous for me
to hear her talk about her rage when fighting a very determined two-year-old, and to imagine the scene she
described as they both shouted and slammed doors. She
didn't know she was the sort of person who did that sort of
thing. She was amazed to find herself going through a
huge spectrum of emotions every day.

Why was she telling me this when I had asked for her
experience of how to grow as a parent on a spiritual path?
Because Buddhism teaches us that awareness is fundamental
and revolutionary. The Buddha has described awareness
as the spiritual path, and awareness starts with ourselves,
knowing ourselves. This apparently ever-tranquil woman
was talking about how much of herself she had simply not
been aware of, had not known, and had never experienced
until she had children. Simply knowing ourselves is a big
step in itself: to be aware of what is going on in our minds,
why we respond as we do, the multiple trains of thoughts
passing through, the underlying stories about who we are
and how we relate to the world, and how they can hold us
back.

children as a mirror

I stopped swearing when my children learned to talk. Before that, I rather enjoyed certain swear words and felt they enriched and broadened my ability to express myself, but I didn't like them when I heard them repeated in the mouths of young children. Children are the perfect mirror, especially in the auditory sense – a fantastic aid to self-awareness. At the simplest level, if I swear, my children swear back. If I back off from a situation out of fear, my children will probably do the same – at least, Jai would probably now lead the way and coax me with helpful encouragement, but I hope you get my point. If I am dissatisfied and complain that things are not right, they complain too. If I respond calmly when someone on the bus is being aggressive, my children will see that meeting aggression with calm is always an option. Children mirror our ways of responding to situations and expressing our preferences, and act as a mirror in which we see our own patterns.

I love it when Ella kisses my forehead. I have always associated such kisses as from parent to child, but having her mirror my behaviour and being the recipient of such kisses is delightful. She also went through a phase of greeting me with 'good morning, gorgeous', which made me smile, lifted my heart, and made me pleased that I had woken her that way for so long. So not all they mirror is bad, by any means. Somehow, I find it harder to identify such concrete ways in which Jai mirrors me, maybe because he is older, and a boy, or more likely because he has always been so strongly his own person. I would like to think that his spontaneous outbursts of gratitude and happiness and awareness of himself in some way reflect aspects of his mother, as well as himself.

Our mental states are reflected by our children; children are so keyed into us. If we argue, I try to question what I'm bringing to it, and whether I was already feeling irritable. In fact, Jai will often pick me up for being impatient or irritable, aware of the inconsistencies in how I respond to him. There aren't very many people in my life who do that. Part of the richness of being a parent is to be challenged a lot, perhaps by children who are sharp and perceptive, know us pretty well, and tell us what they think of us. The challenges may change as our children grow older, but we may find we can't hide from our children the way we sometimes hide from other people.

Their tendency to mirror is just one reason why I believe that children are a gift when it comes to finding out about ourselves and how we respond to situations. If you want to know yourself and learn what it is to be human, without being able to pretend or hide, what better than to have small persons in your life who hold a mirror up to you as you go through the daily, hourly, process of responding to what life throws at you? Children can accelerate the process of self-awareness perhaps faster than we would like to go, not allowing for the luxury of time and a gentle pace. We need to bring compassion to what we see reflected in the mirror and keep a sense of perspective as we learn through that what it means to be human.

I was struck by what I saw in the mirror on a Buddhist retreat one weekend. I was having a conversation about education and how young children learn by imitation, perhaps by seeing their parents absorbed and concentrated in their activities. Later, seated in meditation in the shrine room, this phrase – children learn by imitation – repeated itself in my mind until, with a jolt, I suddenly saw myself as if from outside, mirrored in my children behaving as though they were adults. I remembered my son once describing himself, at the age of 11, as 'stressed', his shoulders too close to his ears from spending too many hours on the computer. I imagined my daughter as an adult, overstretching herself, hoping to be admired and appreciated by her family for managing to bring in a living wage on her own, take responsibility for running the house, and be a 'good' and present parent. And I envisaged her feeling tired, put upon, maybe resentful, sometimes irritable with her own children and partner, perhaps anxious about slow progress in writing a book she had undertaken.... I saw both of them just like their mum – having learned by imitation.

It was like a slap in the face, another wake-up call. I saw clearly how completely irrelevant it was to want them to appreciate or admire me for juggling the practicalities of home and work. I don't want their admiration. What I want is for them to grow up as healthy, happy human beings, embracing life and enjoying the people and the world around them, taking responsibility for making the world a better place, with reasonable expectations of themselves, satisfied with what they choose to do, and dealing with what life throws at them with softness, ease, and receptivity, not tossed from pillar to post and struggling to manage it all. The best chance I can give them is to be a role model, so that they can learn by imitation. What we see in the mirror can be a powerful incentive to live our lives as we would like those we love to live theirs.

This gift of the mirror is not always easy to receive. The calm, neat mother I interviewed said she felt horrible after becoming entrenched in a confrontation with her toddlers, once she realized what she had done and how she was capable of behaving. But she had learned enough not to dwell on mentally beating herself up, to acknowledge that was how she sometimes was, and try to become aware of the consequences. To be able to see ourselves reflected back requires kindly awareness, compassion, and acceptance, and an understanding of what it is to be human – as well as forgiveness.

knowing what presses your buttons

Our reaction to certain behaviours, situations, or words can be automatic and predictable. Sometimes this is likened to a robot controlled by pushbuttons. Press the red one and I shout, the blue one and I smile. Some of my reactions were so predictable that my son soon learned how to press a button or two and get a big reaction. To illustrate the difference between this automatic, reactive way of being – more asleep than awake – and our ability to respond creatively once we introduce awareness and compassion, my Buddhist teacher talks about the 'reactive' mind and the 'creative' mind.[5]

One major button I had when Jai was younger was associated with wilful destruction – his throwing or breaking things during a tantrum. For months, I invariably snapped at such activity, shouting with rage, sometimes holding him with a bit too much force to make him stop, or shaking him (though never hard). In addition to not alleviating the immediate outburst, I always felt terrible about what I had done and couldn't believe I had stooped so low. I would look at my son later, calm and adorable, and be horrified that I had felt such violent rage towards him. I couldn't believe I was capable of such feelings, and I told myself I would never do it again. Yet I still reacted the same way the next time. It felt so strong and I couldn't find a way to stop myself. Even on most objective levels, a child having a tantrum is not a lot of fun, yet there were other quite challenging things that I knew I responded to a lot more helpfully.

Then, one day, awareness kicked in *during* the reaction instead of immediately afterwards, and alongside the inevitable remorse, I clearly saw what was going on and what I had brought to the situation. I saw that this wilful destruction was a particular trigger for me, for whatever reason, and that my son was pressing it at will. I saw with horrifying clarity the extent to which my actions and my emotions were being determined by my four-year-old child. That realization made my toes curl, and it still does.

In Buddhism, this toe-curling is known as positive humiliation. It was quite a turning point for me to see that red button activated by my son. In the end, that is what changed my behaviour. Once I fully realized that, and felt in my guts the humiliation of knowing that I was predictably activated by a small child, I did stop reacting in those situations. A little voice reached me through the rage which said, 'This is just the sort of thing you react to, and you know the consequences of reacting.' I found myself quietly saying, 'I'm going to go away and leave you to do this, and when you've finished I will make you pick up everything you threw.' As well as not having to deal with the consequences of my violent reactions – remorse, guilt, an upset child – this had the wonderful added consequence of removing that particular trigger. My clever son quickly learned not to bother.

Another classic button, according to one parent of teenagers, is, 'Mum, you just don't understand!' She could too easily have a good shouting match after a comment like that. One mother described how raw she felt when her daughter was 15 and 16, when she just did what she wanted and could be very difficult. It reminded her of when she was in the so-called terrible twos. She was taken by surprise by the anger she felt at being hurt and baffled. The rawness arose because her daughter knew her and wanted to press buttons. For the mother, there was a process of realizing what was happening, seeing how she was reacting, and realizing that she had to work with her own reactions. It was not just about communicating with her daughter, but also about understanding her emotional responses.

Knowing ourselves is crucial, so that we can recognize what is happening and catch ourselves starting to react. This includes awareness of who we are and our tendencies

– the buttons we have and how we react when they are pressed. In my view, we don't even need to understand *why* we have certain reactions and responses, just know they are there. When we understand our reactions and what triggers them, we are more able to move from not having a choice – from the reactive mind – to having a choice about how we respond to that particular trigger. We don't have to take things personally and react defensively to whatever comes our way. Once we see the dynamic and know the triggers, we have the opportunity to respond more positively and helpfully, with a creative mind. Changing these responses takes time, but with awareness we edge closer and closer and are able one day to catch ourselves before we do or say things we would rather not. When your teenager accuses you of just not understanding, and you know it is an easy trap to avoid, you then have a choice about whether to shout back, drop it, ask a question, or make a comment that moves things forward.

knowing how you are in the moment

I may be waiting at the school gate or in a work situation when someone asks, 'How are you?' and I say 'Fine.' It is an automatic response and probably as much detail as the questioner actually wants to hear. Answering that way sometimes makes me aware that I don't really know how I am. But I know exactly how I am by how I respond with my children. I may have low-lying irritability or unhappiness that I can keep covered or be unaware of in most situations, but put me with my children and I will suddenly and unexpectedly feel overwhelmed and exhausted when they don't do what I want them to, or I lose my temper and snap at them. That is when I know how I am: that I am *not* fine. Or I might be feeling fairly neutral, but when pushed, my response is light and expansive, able to meet what my children chuck my way and respond creatively. Either way, being with children can be an authenticity check that removes any veneer and ensures that how we are is real.

I have a friend who has run Buddhist family retreats for many years. A father himself, he has often said that he believes all those considering themselves good, calm Buddhists should spend at least some time in the company of two- or three-year-olds, or help out on a family retreat. His belief is that this would cut through any possibility of people being lulled into a false sense of security, imagining that they can patiently and skilfully negotiate all that life throws at them. Being with young children is, in his view, an excellent test of patience and soon shows what people are like. In many situations, it can be easy for me to kid myself that I am doing well and I am not getting caught up in negative emotions, until after school. Or I may simply be feeling quite calm and find my children bringing out a ready playfulness, tapping into an underlying stability and happiness that I had not been aware of. Being with children keeps me on that cutting edge.

I think it is always good to know how I am, at least roughly. I don't want or need to dwell on my every emotion or analyse why it is there, but I know from experience that I generally have a much greater connection with others and behave in a more positive way, and more authentically, when I am not cut off from how I am. Also, once we know what's going on, that gives us the essential small space to pause and choose how to respond. For example, if I know that I am close to the edge and feeling under pressure, I can switch on a mental warning bell and consider that I need to be careful and possibly a bit more protective of myself. It may be caused by being premenstrual, tired, or worried about work deadlines, and my warning bell tells me that I am more likely to respond badly to my children or other people, neither of which I want to do. If I am reasonably OK and grounded, I can relax more, trusting myself to respond appropriately whatever happens, more flexible and open to what the day brings.

If you do catch yourself snapping unexpectedly or feeling neutral, you can try the techniques described in earlier chapters in relation to bringing awareness to fear or resentment. Try following your breath for just three breaths, in and out. Open curiosity can then be very helpful. See if you can locate physical sensations in different parts of your body associated with those feelings or emotions. Just try to notice the thoughts in your head, labelling them if it helps – worrying, planning, or fantasizing, for example. There is no need to ask why a feeling or thought is there, just notice it. Nor do you necessarily need quiet or space to do this – a playground or checkout queue is fine, as long as you are not actually engaged in conversation. There are likely to be several things going on at the same time, some of which may be painful, others pleasurable, and others neutral. You may find that as you bring your attention to them, some of them change or dissolve. Sometimes I notice just how immensely trivial or insubstantial most of it actually is, even those thoughts masquerading as serious or deeply important. All this can help in taking oneself that bit more lightly.

patterns in your own upbringing

It is only by becoming conscious of how we respond that we can free ourselves from our conditioning and make our own choices. Our main source of information and experience on how to be a parent comes from how we ourselves were parented. Without awareness of ourselves and the choices we have, there is a very strong tendency to either repeat what was done to us or react against it and attempt to do the opposite. If we question ourselves, perhaps we do so because of books or friends, or theories about parenting or fear of criticism. If we are lucky, the blueprint from how we were parented is largely helpful and positive. Even then, an unconscious rerun will not help us to be aware of ourselves or to grow spiritually through awareness of ourselves and what it is to be human.

Retreats and other times away have helped me to see some
of the patterns I have inherited from how I was parented.
One recurrent theme has been, 'I am not Superwoman and
I must stop pretending I am.' Actually, that one started
with anxiety about going home at the end of a retreat and
thinking, 'Other people must stop assuming I am Superwoman and can do everything.' The first shift was to take
more responsibility for my expectations of myself and seeing where they came from. My mother started a business
when the four of us were young children. She was always
there when we were tiny, and later for school runs, and a
solid presence in the kitchen while we did our homework.
She worked during school hours and then again at night,
not infrequently until three in the morning. I did the same
for years, pushing myself to combine work and motherhood without compromising. It is not usually difficult to
trace these patterns. It is harder to shift the unhelpful ones,
but becoming aware of them is the first step.

Being a parent naturally helps us reflect on our own life
and childhood. It comes up automatically when we find
ourselves saying what our parents said to us. 'O what a tan-
gled web we weave, when first we practise to deceive,' is an
example of a favourite quotation of my mother's that I use,
along with promising my children that if they tell the truth
they can avoid punishment, and praising them for not
lying. As my son drifts towards adolescence, sometimes
silently hiding behind a long fringe of hair, at other times
charmingly open and communicative, I hear my mother's
voice in my head, 'Just keep them talking, darling, keep
them talking,' emphasizing the importance of listening
now to help ensure my children still talk to me in their
teens and beyond. These are all helpful habits and I have
chosen to mirror them in my own parenting. Yet there are
other things I have chosen to do differently from my own
upbringing.

I have friends who grew up with anxious parents, or whose mother or father was constantly critical of the world. It can be more of a challenge to free ourselves from these and other more powerful or negative constructions from the past. Whatever the parenting, however helpful or unhelpful, when it comes to growing in awareness, the key is simply to become aware of what they are and how we have responded to them, what we have copied and what we have negated, and to be aware of ourselves and our aspirations. It is not that we have either to accept or reject the gifts of our parents. Nor do we need to try to analyse why our parents behaved as they did, or apportion blame. Most parents do the best they can with the resources available – emotional, financial, spiritual, and intellectual. The point is simply to be aware of our legacy from our own parents when we fumble around learning to be parents ourselves, so that we get to know ourselves better and have more choice about what gifts we do and don't accept, and how to find our own way as a parent, gradually and kindly.

the stories you tell yourself

In Chapter 2, we saw how, according to the Buddha's teaching of the two arrows, we might feel we have been struck by one arrow when we have in fact been hit by two. Children can often be the first arrow, and if we learn to distinguish between the two arrows we can see how much of what is going on in our minds is actually the second arrow, the stories we tell ourselves rather than the immediate reality of what has happened. We might be upset by something our child has done, but instead of focusing on that, we pile other bits on top of it. For example, one day halfway through his first term at secondary school, my son didn't come home from school. That was the first arrow and it hit me hard as I phoned friends, drove around trying to find him, and wondered when I should involve the police. He turned up well before dark, cheerful after a good time with his friends, genuinely and positively heard my anxiety, and took on board that he should have phoned me. But the second arrow had seen him becoming a vandal, hanging out with shoplifters, slipping out of my grasp, the end of childhood and the beginning of a difficult adolescence. That arrow proved much harder to remove, even though the first never struck again and all indications are that he is turning out to be both streetwise and reasonably responsible.

During one group discussion about parenting and spiritual practice, one mother was recounting how she found herself becoming disgruntled at the end of each day. When her husband came home in the evenings, she would tell him at length about the difficulties she'd had with their young son, such as the struggles to get him to put his shoes on, or a tantrum in the park. She thought it would help to share them, but she noticed that instead of making her feel better, sharing the frustrating parts of the day made her relive them and made them longer, rather than fairly short periods over the course of the day. Across the room from her was a single mother who listened and then leaned forward, describing how what she really missed in not having a co-parent was not being able to share the joys and small achievements of her daughter during the day, not having another adult in her life who could be interested and proud when her daughter shared something with a friend or put on her own shoes.

The first mother instantly saw how her thoughts were focused on the difficult rather than the delightful, and she resolved on the spot to find the good moments in each day and instead share those with her husband each evening. For her, bringing her thoughts into the light of day had helped her to see what was going on in her mind, and that she had a choice whether to follow the thoughts that were loudest or simply to let them be there and draw out the quieter ones.

A friend of mine recently had her first baby – a delightfully cheerful and appealing five-month-old girl by the time I met her. However, my friend had had a very hard time since the birth. She'd read the latest book on how to raise a baby and tried unsuccessfully to encourage her to fit the sleep and other patterns it advocated. She had, in her opinion, completely failed, and she felt miserable about it. After she eventually gave up trying, her baby daughter turned into a model baby but, more importantly, my friend stopped expecting to be a perfect mother and know exactly what to do every time. She was learning perfectly adequately from experience. The story in her head from what the book said lost its power, and she became better at hearing her own voice.

In this way, awareness of our thoughts can help us identify where they have come from. We might see that many of the stories we tell ourselves, or the benchmarks against which we measure ourselves, are put there by other people or the prevailing ideas about right and wrong. This in turn can make it easier to let those thoughts just pass through and wander away, without giving them any power or leaping after them like a dog following the trail of every scent. In the end, there is no one specific right or wrong way to bring up children. Maybe what we need most is reassurance and confidence, to trust ourselves to be 'good enough' parents and not worry about getting it exactly right every time.

Deciding on a secondary school can be difficult, and a key time in which to unpick the source of contradictory thoughts. I knew what was important to me: that my children could go to school locally, have local friends, experience the mixed community, do well enough to get to university, and avoid being knifed. That should have made the whole process reasonably easy, living as we do in an inner London borough. In fact, it didn't leave a lot of choice. There was just one school, to be precise, at least for my son. But instead, I went through paroxysms of doubt and insecurity for months, oscillating as to whether to move house, and whether Jai should sit exams for selective schools. I was surrounded by parents tutoring their children, anxiety about entrance exams, and people suggesting that I was failing my intelligent son by not giving him the opportunity to excel academically through selective schooling.

Once I reconnected with what was originally most important to me, and stopped engaging with the many ideas from other parents, friends, and family, there really was no choice – just that one school – and the stress evaporated. Being aware of the different storylines can enable us to step back a bit and see where they've come from. This often removes their potency. Then we can have more say over the extent to which we base our lives on those storylines or our own intuition and values.

an opportunity to break the mould

Have you ever found yourself saying, 'I'm not the sort of person who does that,' or 'That's just who I am, I've always done it that way'? Even a negative self-image can give a sense of safety, defining who we are and who we are not and how we fit within the world. We may even aspire to be different but feel stuck and limited by how we perceive our own potential. Or else, as I have done several times, we simply find a way of being that works for us most of the time. We don't often feel vulnerable or threatened, we feel reasonably content, and we can cope with most things we encounter, so there is no need to change. Yet the stories we have about what we do or don't do are just stories. Ultimately, they have little or no substance. I remember a friend of mine telling me how her brother's favourite phrases included 'A leopard can't change its spots,' and 'I'm too old to change,' yet her experience of him was that he had already changed dramatically when, in his forties, he became a father.

Being a parent can rock the foundations of a carefully constructed self-image, and rock those foundations it should. However much we like that image and feel safe within it, or however much we dislike it, it is not real, because we all change. It is also limiting. While we are fixed, we cannot grow. Some people describe becoming a parent as shattering, like a shell breaking into pieces. Having a hard outer shell would keep us fixed, limiting our growth. The shattering creates gaps and an opportunity to rearrange the pieces. This is an opportunity for growth. We are so much more than our experience of ourselves, with infinitely greater potential. What could be more liberating than to feel the cracks in a fixed self view opening up, with air coming in giving us space to breathe and to grow?

One of the reasons children can be so helpful in shattering this shell is that, when we become parents, we have unfamiliar emotions and other new experiences. That helped to shake up my view of myself. At work, I know I usually come across as calm, self-possessed, and positive. There is usually very little to shake that. But as a parent I know that the person my colleagues and clients see is only part of the picture – probably the middle bit. All around that middle range of feelings and emotions I have the potential to respond with a love and joy that brings tears to my eyes, to react with enormous frustration and rage, regress to being locked into a childish argument, or display peace-keeping abilities that are simply not required of me in most other aspects of my life.

As parents, we might feel shocked by the rage that surfaces to meet a determined toddler, the frustration at a crying baby that won't explain what it wants, the sheer strength of our emotions, or the emotional range that we can experience during the day. We normally experience a familiar set of emotions. We might remain blissfully unaware of the anger of which we are capable until we try to raise children; we might also not realize the depth of love of which we are capable. As one parent eloquently put it during an interview, 'Children make sure – by being very good at pushing our buttons and reflecting back our rather more negative sides – that we don't retain grand ideas about ourselves. A spiritual friend or one's worst enemy rarely matches the unbounded challenge of a disgruntled teenager or a toddler in a tantrum.'

Challenging our view of who we are can loosen preconceptions or assumptions we might have held since childhood, some of which turn out to have very flimsy foundations. Whether it is those who 'aren't musical' learning the piano for the first time alongside their children, or learning to say, 'I love you,' even though your parents never did so, loosening up who we are, and what we can do, can feel scary at times, but it can also be an exciting way of expanding our horizons. The shattering effect of the rapid change into which many new parents are catapulted can provide a flexibility in who we are. This offers an opportunity to remain less fixed, to keep the pieces more fluid, to allow our experience of ourselves falling apart and rearranging, rather than trying to find a new self-image as a parent into which to fix ourselves as quickly as possible.

dealing with the bits you don't like

Do you ever think it is only you who feels unable to cope, or that most people manage better than you? Or that everyone else is overflowing with unconditional love and generosity while you struggle with resentment? In the clear light of day, I find it impossible to conceive of violent rage towards my children, even when I know that I have been angry with them. I have so many unpleasant thoughts and feelings that don't fit with how I aspire to be. But these thoughts and feelings don't define me any more than the more positive and spiritual ones, the ones I approve and want to be associated with. And the most wonderful thing to me about being aware of our heights and depths is that once we know what is there, we can deal with it and move on, instead of finding it slips out in different ways and never really seeing it for what it is.

I recently went through a period of strong rage, fairly consistently, over a period of about three months. It took me by surprise and ran completely counter to my reasonable, tolerant, easygoing self-image. For the first two months I hated it, so I effectively made my experience even worse by bitterly resenting the rage – and the causes of it – for taking up so much of my head space and making me feel tight and uncomfortable. I piled on the pain even more by being critical of myself for not being able to shift it. What good were sixteen years of meditation if I couldn't escape the endless, circular, furious thoughts? I had enough awareness to know that I needed to be very careful indeed and wait for the rage to pass before making decisions or taking action, so I did manage some effective damage limitation. However, I felt horrible.

Eventually, through the red fog, I remembered the suggestions and techniques I have described in these pages, including turning towards strong emotions rather than suppressing them – which simply doesn't work – and the value of curiosity. I decided to put them into practice. I consciously said to myself, 'Wow! Isn't it interesting, suddenly feeling so much rage, after all these years,' and I sat quietly, alone and upright, and took my attention through my body, scanning different parts and trying to identify and locate different physical sensations. At first, it seemed there was nothing there except the all-consuming rage. I started looking more closely at the exact location of the physical feelings, and asking what rage actually felt like in my body – whether it was hot, cold, tight, or numb – and trying to identify the associated thoughts.

Within the first half hour, I started to come across physical sensations that were nothing to do with the rage, and I noticed thoughts about completely unrelated things. When I took my attention to the angry thoughts and just named them – 'Angry thought … oh whoops, there goes another angry thought,' – they dissolved or became more elusive. I found myself getting distracted surprisingly quickly, my mind wandering onto other stories which were nothing to do with the rage. That was the beginning of the end of that rage. It took a few more weeks for it to subside completely, and I took my awareness to it every time it threatened to take over again, but each time it returned it was weaker, and my mind drifted to other things more quickly.

In retrospect, I am really pleased that rage did surface. It left me with clearer boundaries and I marvelled again at the almost magical effect of simply bringing a curious, kindly awareness to whatever was going on. If you don't already do that, I would strongly recommend giving it a go. Even feelings of anger, jealousy, or self-pity can change, shift, and lose their power under the gaze of this kindly curiosity. It is safe to assume that what arises for us is not unique and has probably been thought or felt thousands of times by billions of parents. You are not a uniquely useless or horrible person. Nor am I, or anyone else I know.

Once we know what feelings and emotions arise, and are no longer taken by surprise by them, we have an opportunity to learn to sit with an emotion, let it just be there, and feel it rather than act on it. By learning more about who we are, about our heights and our depths, we can gradually learn to open up to strong feelings and let ourselves feel them. It is wonderful to be able to feel really strongly without the fear of being so overwhelmed that we lose control and do something damaging or unhelpful. I find this liberating at a very deep level. It liberates me from being governed by my emotions, feelings, and thoughts – whether positive or negative. However strong the emotion, we have a choice about how to respond.

Greater familiarity with the wide range of emotions of which we are capable also opens an opportunity to reflect on what it is to be human, and to be honest and real about this without hiding behind a façade of nice, easy emotions. Through being aware of ourselves and what it means to be human, we can get more deeply in touch with the fact that we share with everybody a huge amount of emotional and visceral experience. We learn more about ourselves through being a parent, and through this we learn about life and what it is to be human.

Throughout this roller-coaster journey of self-awareness, we need to take each bump and turn within the context of it being a spiritual journey. Self-awareness is crucial because it is the first aspect of awareness, and awareness is the spiritual life. To open more and more to awareness includes the need for self-awareness; not necessarily lots of questions or analysis about why we feel certain emotions or have particular thoughts, but a certain level of self-awareness. Raising children provides fabulous opportunities to get to know ourselves more fully and authentically. It is one of the great opportunities open to us as parents. Throughout that journey, we need to hold ourselves and our experience with the same kindly awareness we use to explore particular aspects of our humanness, and treat ourselves with compassion, tolerance, forgiveness, and as much patience as we can muster.

4

growing through insights

This is a short extract from an email I wrote to a friend and mentor some years ago, describing some reflections as I waited for the kettle to boil one evening. It was one of the seeds that germinated to become this book.

It is 9.30 in the evening. I have been delousing my children – again. What is it now – eight, maybe nine, years of combing hair? I am very tired, and quite low with the tiredness. I am reminded of a Greek myth featuring gods whose names I can't remember. One god is sentenced to an eternity of pushing a boulder uphill. As soon as he gets to the top, the boulder rolls back to the bottom and he has to start again. As soon as I am about to break the breeding cycle of the common head louse, my children rest their head against that of another child in their class, or they go to their father's for a few comb-free days, and we have another infestation. It is grindingly repetitive, continuous, never-ending.

Except, of course, that it isn't. As the kettle boils I reflect on how Jai's head of almost white-blond curls has given way to almost straight brown hair, the once unmanageable mane cut neatly into something that will avoid standing out and teasing at school. Ella's early frizz that matted at the slightest breeze is unrecognizable, now beautifully thick, long brown hair, usually in two plaits as mine was at her age. Instead of the uncomprehending screams of protest at this unjust torture from someone who was supposed to love them, they both engage with the combing. They alert me if their head is itchy. Jai enjoys the attention of being groomed, and Ella combs half her head while I do the rest. We marvel at the quantity, size, or, tonight, the sparseness of the crop. I tell them how much lice appreciate clean hair, destigmatizing the affair the same way my mother did, to avoid the further discomfort of my children's neurotic reactions to the little creatures.

Not long after I wrote this email, Jai locked me out of the bathroom and took responsibility for his own hair, now long and unruly again – and lice-free. Their father had long since got on the case with a louse comb, but this experience stayed with me. It is one example of a small, felt experience of – or insight into – the essence of Buddhism. The Buddha's first conceptual description of his Enlightenment experience as recorded in the Pali Canon says,

This being, that becomes;
from the arising of this, that arises;
this not becoming, that does not become;
from the ceasing of this, that ceases.[6]

In other words, everything is conditional on something else, or on complex combinations of things, so nothing and no one is either completely independent or permanent. Instead, we live amidst a constant flow of cause and effect, arising and falling away, of one generation of head lice after another.... This is the law of conditioned co-production and is the foundation of all Buddhist teachings, a common ground for all schools of Buddhism. The whole of Buddhism can be seen as attempt to communicate this vision, what this means for how we live our lives, and how we too can become Enlightened.

the reality of impermanence

This can all seem quite obvious at first glance. Yet after his Enlightenment under the bodhi tree at Bodh Gaya in India, the Buddha hesitated to communicate the truth he had realized, thinking it could not be fully understood using concepts or intellect. Even if it does sound logical intellectually, look a little closer. Do you respond to everything you encounter from this basis? It is one thing to read conceptual descriptions and reflect on cause and effect. It is another to have these ideas deeply affect the way we live our lives.

As an older friend of mine put it so eloquently, she can embrace the reality of impermanence as she watches leaves fall from the trees, but contemplating her own death terrifies her. On a much smaller level, I know in theory that my computer is not permanent, that it will go wrong and wear out. But you'd be hard pressed to recognize that if you saw the extent of my indignation and disbelief when it doesn't work properly. You might have experienced similar reactions to a car that won't start or a punctured bicycle tyre. We are told that the Buddha's spiritual experience of 'seeing things as they really are' transformed his entire being. We live surrounded by the reality of change and impermanence, yet we only absorb it on a certain level. In order to grow spiritually, Buddhism teaches us that we need to realize this reality at deeper and deeper levels, so that it actually shifts the ways we relate to life, bit by bit. That is why insights are so helpful.

Experiences such as the head lice combing did shift something in me, and it can still affect how I respond in small ways. When I am in a similar situation and my mind is telling me that what I am facing is endless, that experience sometimes pops up in my memory and reminds me that, no, it may feel that way, but it is not endless, nothing is, it will shift. I can place my immediate frustration in a broader context and get more of a sense of the change and the cause and effect inherent within it. As with most things to do with children, it will change pretty quickly – not necessarily for the better, but it will change. This reminder can also help how I respond in the moment, encouraging me to hold more lightly to whatever it is that feels so endless.

Insights tend to be a felt experience, realizations that may be felt in our bodies as well as an 'ah-ha!' moment in our mind. They may often be accompanied by lightness or joy. By the time the kettle boiled that evening, I was smiling to myself, the weariness and pressure having evaporated, and I almost laughed. From that new perspective, there suddenly seemed to be something faintly ridiculous in becoming so lost and entrenched in one small moment that it was all I could see and became my reality. Stepping back, I could see the flow and change of life not only through the trying fact that one louse can lay hundreds of eggs, but also contact the fact that my mother – and countless generations before her – went through the same process, and that my practical, non-neurotic response to lice was so directly influenced by hers, which gave rise to love for her. The image of my children's changing heads of hair inspired love for them and the preciousness of each brief stage of their lives. Something about experiencing myself and my children's lice as part of a bigger picture, arising and passing for generations, was what brought on that lightness.

Raising children is full of precious opportunities to live close to the reality of impermanence and open ourselves to the possibility of insights that transform us, tiny bit by tiny bit, in our heights and our depths, and in the ways we respond to the world. We all have these moments of felt experiences, of insights, though sometimes we might not recognize or value them. Making a note of them can help, whether in a journal or an email. We can also consciously open ourselves to opportunities for insight by bringing ourselves face to face with how things constantly change.

We might notice aspects of the cause and effect of some of our experiences and, when we have a few moments, reflect on them, seeing how what is immediately in front of us is part of a bigger picture. Or, rather than mental reflection, we might notice how we feel in our bodies when facing this flow of change, and try to take this truth on board by feeling it in our guts, with the awareness that we are aiming to live our lives based on that awareness.

When my children were small, I got used to the fact that as soon as I had found a pat answer to describe one stage of development, they had moved on and I found myself having to change the description. It's not very different even now. Children simply do not stay the same. Neither do I, of course, and nor do my friends or family, but our development is slower and reminds me of impermanence less often than my children.

Another mother I interviewed talked about how her family would regularly reach a stage where she thought they had it all sorted; they had a nice routine and everything was great. Then her sons would grow a bit more, their comfortable routine suddenly no longer worked, and they had to find a new one. Sometimes there are big changes, such as a child starting school or leaving home. There are also lots of smaller opportunities to notice change. Some parents said living with teenagers helped them be aware that experiences are fluid by watching how rapidly their children's moods changed.

Opportunities to notice how things change can arise even before our children are born. I have several friends who had their first child in their early forties. They were long-awaited and much-wanted babies. One such friend, pregnant at last, had an anxious time with scares about miscarriage throughout her pregnancy. She watched things change from hour to hour, including her fear of losing the baby. She felt as though it was the first time she had consciously observed impermanence within herself from moment to moment. Her thoughts, moods, and feelings had swung around before, but never in such a rapid succession, and never before had she kept so still to watch them. At times, she recounted finding a deep sense of contentment in watching the speed of change, and the rise and fall of her emotions, moving from intense anxiety and fear to acceptance and calm, knowing that however bad she felt at a given moment, it would not last, just as the periods of relief where the risk seemed to subside also passed.

By the time this book was in its second draft, this friend and her husband had two healthy children. While she may have less time to sit still and watch the changes in her thoughts and feelings, a felt experience of this sort does stay with us, especially if we recognize that what we are seeing is part of a flow and change that happens all the time, for everyone. We can bring this to mind when we feel stuck. Through immersing ourselves in impermanence, we can move more and more towards a state in which we don't just believe in the concept that everything is subject to change, but become an increasingly more willing and conscious part of that change, of the constant flow of life. The more we live with this awareness, the more we effectively step back and allow our view to become more expansive, and the more we can see the extent of this truth all around us. And the more we see this web of cause and effect, the better we are able to make choices based on how things actually are.

living with the fear of death

A particularly vivid image was painted for me by one friend when she described the simple daily task of emptying the dishwasher while heavily pregnant with her first child. Whenever she learned over, she became uncomfortably aware of the the knives and forks pointing up from the cutlery holder towards the large bump of her belly.

Logically, she knew there was no danger, but she was shocked to realize that she was concerned for her baby's safety before it had even been born. In that moment, she realized she might feel that fear for the rest of her life, that fear of death and loss was an integral part of being a parent.

Despite the fact that her own two sons were long since grown up and left home, another mother I interviewed vividly recalled how she was struck by an awareness of mortality when her first child was four days old. It was the middle of the night and she was very tired. She had picked him up and walked him up and down to get him back to sleep. She felt a sudden flash of anger towards him for not letting her sleep, then the shock of the realization, 'He is mortal. He will die.' It struck her as strange that this hadn't occurred to her until her children were born. It wasn't just an intellectual thought, but a felt experience in her body, and an insight into that reality. She understood that the realization came in the wake of a flash of anger because she became aware of her son's vulnerability. Her next thought was, 'What have I done?' She had no idea what she was opening herself up to by choosing to have children, the magnitude of the potential loss, and the effect that might have on her. The question was how to face that and live the rest of her life with the possibility of that potential loss. It was that question that set her on a quest that led her to Buddhism. While she did not believe she had found an answer when I interviewed her more than thirty years later, she saw the question as a spur to growth: to be able to hold the question and live with the reality of loving someone who would one day die.

So how is that helpful? How can becoming more aware of death help anyone? Does spiritual progress mean aspiring to a state in which it would be fine if one of our children died before us? Not at all. But when we shut out any aspect of life, we close down to much more than that one aspect. Death is part of life. Selective awareness doesn't really

work. It just does not work like that, at least not over time –
though I must admit I sometimes fervently wish it did. The
more of life and our experience we push away from ourselves, the harder it becomes to open and embrace any
aspect of life.

As I write this, I am looking at the last of the November
colours in a beautiful Essex woodland, enjoying the leaves
on the ground, and nudging at the edge of my awareness is
the fact that leaves are not the only things that die. Head
lice have a life cycle of about two weeks, leaves fall once a
year, the nearby rabbits live perhaps five years, our cats
maybe twenty years if they are lucky and careful, and
people, well, getting longer and longer, it seems, but still a
finite life cycle. Yet life goes on. The times when we feel
more expansive and calmer are opportunities to acknowledge our fear of death and the reality of loss and hold
them within a bigger perspective.

Sometimes it seems as if the line between our children
being alive or dead is far too thin. One moment they are
holding our hands to cross the road and we may have fearful images of them running out in the path of an oncoming
car. Your own child might once have had an accident, or
you might have gone through a process of torturing yourself with thoughts of a near miss or what might have happened. As parents, we do tend to think about the death of
children because we fear it, and that is why being a parent
provides such ample opportunities to contemplate death
and to bring awareness to the effect that has on us. I came
across a copy of a letter I wrote to a friend when Jai was a
baby. She had her first child a few months later, and must
have written to me describing how she was living in fear
that her healthy newborn baby would simply stop breathing. In my reply, I wrote,

*Dear Carolyn, Just before reading your letter I had
gone in to check Jai was still breathing. (He is.) I don't*

check as often as I used to, but I still check a lot. Someone recently said to me, 'Of course, you feel so vulnerable being a parent,' and that summed it all up for me. Welcome to the world of never (again?) being able to control happiness. More than ever before, there is now someone else on which that depends. That's what I feel anyway. Sometimes I am philosophical and think what it would be like if Jai died, and I think at least he would never have become disillusioned with the world and with human nature, that he has had a happy seven-and-a-half months thinking everyone is nice and loves him. But, as you can see, it is at front of my mind, and even the thought makes me cry and I don't think we're alone. It's just a part of life now.

I doubt whether I really could control my happiness before I had Jai, but maybe that was the first time I became conscious just how little control I do have. Parents share an experience of extreme terror of losing someone that might not apply to the same degree in other relationships. Yet, at least sometimes, I want to try to stay open, not shut down and push away those fears, because I want to be able to stay present and open to life in all its richness. That includes trying, bit by bit, to hold the reality of death as part of life. If you have the opportunity to be aware of the feelings in your body, you might catch the contracting effect in the area around your heart when this fear arises. You can try consciously bringing a kindly curiosity to the feelings in your body, or thoughts in your head, when fear is present, just noticing them without judging. You might, like my friend, notice how feelings shift, and the associated relaxation and openness in your body if there is more trust and acceptance in your experience.

An increased fear of death does not automatically lead to spiritual growth, of course. Like so many of the opportunities presented by parenting, there is a potential pitfall. The danger is that we become even more likely to shut down to the world around us, to protect our family unit, and try to control our environment to give us a sense of security and certainty. Once again, it is what we do with our awareness and how we respond to it that counts. We can let awareness of death remind us that life does not last for ever, and that we should make the most of our precious time, appreciate the people in our lives, and simply sit with how difficult it feels to hold both love and the awareness that life is finite.

Our children's mortality can feel unbearable. To live with that awareness can have a strong effect. We are not aiming to reach a point at which we do not care if our children suffer and die, but for a deep and pure response of love and compassion. True compassion arises when a loving heart meets suffering. It is infinitely powerful and not clouded by blame, indignation, disbelief, or lack of acceptance. We are aiming to love at the same time as taking in – on deeper and deeper levels – the reality that everyone we love will one day die.

Having children can also put us in touch with our own mortality. Our own life suddenly matters more, because someone else is dependent on us, or so it seems. I have cycled around London for many years, but it was not until my first child was born that I started to wear a helmet. I used to curse when I had near misses, but over the years I trained my response to a more moderate shout of 'Be careful!' because having people swear back at me is pretty unpleasant. However, I realized something had shifted in me one day as I swerved to avoid a car and, without thinking, shouted, 'Oi! My life is precious too!' The proximity of death, if only in our fears, provides us with an opportunity to embrace life and its preciousness. Every life is precious; ours too. This is true before we have children, and it is no less true for non-parents, yet as parents we can use the fact that death may be present in our minds to make us more aware of the preciousness of human life.

letting go of the desire to be in control

Cycling along the road behind Ella epitomizes what it feels like not to be in control. I find it almost unbearable. I have to trust her and what she has been taught: that she will stop at the crossroads, and that she will remain upright. I need to have at least some faith that other people will obey the rules of the road. I minimize the times I shout words of caution, for fear of making her anxious or putting her off cycling. But I hate it and my stomach is in knots. I love the fact that she can cycle and I want her to enjoy it and improve. I choose quiet roads and I stay close, yet I can hardly wait to get her home to a safer environment.

For many parents I interviewed, one of the major effects of having a child was to find themselves in a world in which they were no longer in control. Or rather, they became conscious, for the first time, of the extent to which they were not in control. Beforehand, they may have had an illusion of control, doing things when they felt like it and delivering what they had promised on time. Children provide good opportunities for removing the illusion of control over one's life, such as choosing when to sleep, when to go out, when to have quiet time, and what to spend money on.

This may not sound positive, but it is! Life is king, and that is not what we want. We want to control what we cannot. Things come into being and change in dependence on conditions, and few or none or those conditions are within our direct control. So surely it is better to have our nose pressed against that sometimes unsavoury reality than to go through the years kidding ourselves that we can go on controlling our immediate environment so that it works for us.

We can approach anything with a desire to control, even meditation. The desire to control creeps into our spiritual life as well. It is an instinctual human response to the wish to feel secure. It is the reactive, grasping, smaller self that wants to hold things and reject things, and tries to control what happens. This doesn't work in the long run. It doesn't help us to grow, doesn't help us to let go into life and embrace it with a solidity and expansiveness that is not dependent on illusions of security. We are trying to encourage the more creative, flexible responses. There is also the danger that the illusion of control will come crashing down all at once and be even harder to deal with.

Because I know this, I smile at myself when I accompany Ella on bike rides. I smile at the knots in my stomach and my urgency to get her safely home, because I believe that, on some level of which I cannot be fully conscious, it is helpful to be in a situation where I feel vulnerable and not in full control, and simply deal with it – or at least bear it – moment by moment. Simply by not aborting the whole trip or shouting ahead too often, I am opening myself to just being in an environment in which I am aware of my lack of complete control, and I have faith that, on some subtle level, putting myself in that situation is eroding that small part of me that wants to organize and control, and shut out the bits of life that threaten me and avoid feeling vulnerable. It is also giving Ella the space she needs to grow in confidence and become her own person. I want her to be able to grow too, and that helps reinforce my need to loosen my grip. If we close down to the bits of life we don't feel safe with, we close down to other aspects too. We open ourselves to the opportunity for insight when we accept and live with awareness of the lack of control we do have, slowly allowing that to transform us. So as I cycle with Ella, I choose to feel the knots, and crank myself a little more open to life.

At those times when I do feel more open, enjoying and trusting life, I feel more in contact with the force for good that is so much a part of this arising and falling, coming together and ceasing. In Buddhism, this is sometimes conceptualized as the universal will to Enlightenment, the awakened heart, or *bodhicitta*. Some people connect more with images of universal love or grace waves – a positive flow that is there all the time, even when we are not in contact with it. When I resist the natural changes and flow of life, it is like swimming against the stream; when I relax and accept my lack of control, I feel I align myself more with the flow and get carried along. Of course we protect our children, and we shouldn't let go of that responsibility or desire. But this awareness of the flow of life can sometimes help me to let go, and see not only that we cannot control everything, but that we don't have to, and it may even be better when we don't.

After I had let go of my daughter in the river I mentioned in Chapter 2, and then got in the river myself, an image occurred to me that made me smile. When I'm resisting the natural flow of life, it is like struggling to stand in white water against the powerful current, and banging my head against the huge rock that was in front of me. I spend too much time doing that. My helmet gives me some protection, but it is still hard work, and all I really need to do is lie back and trust the water to take me the easy way around the rock. It is almost as if we can sit back and let things be, and not try to control everything. We can't hope to control everything anyway, and as long as we are open to aligning ourselves with something positive in the world, that is fine. We can then let ourselves be carried along in a positive direction, better able to make positive choices. Life is not about scrambling up river all the time. When I am in touch with this force for good, the effect is one of making less effort, having more energy, and finding it easier to let go of the need to be in control.

Being divorced and living apart from my children's father has meant that I have to let go and trust someone else. Well, I have to let the children go physically, and if I did not also trust, I would drive myself crazy with anxiety when they were away, unable to benefit from the space that gives me. I did that at first, and I still have anxieties, but I have mostly learned to let go. I did this because I had to, but I have since realized how immensely valuable that has been in enabling me to make the best use of my time apart from my children. Without that time in which to write, this book would never have got beyond a vague idea. I still feel bereft when they leave me, every other Friday, but I register the feelings of anxiety or loss and choose not to give them further time, leaving me freer to enjoy the space. No doubt you also have time on your own which you can choose to spend worrying, or being creative.

On a similar note, I have watched friends struggling with the fact that their partner and co-parent does things differently, and they have different views when it comes to raising children, or different boundaries or rules. I notice this particularly with babies and young children. There is a place, of course, for discussion and negotiation, and most of the couples I know have reached compromises over time. But perhaps there is also scope for consciously letting go of things being done the way you like them all the time. This is also true when parents live separately but are both involved in raising their children. They may have even more differences in how things should be done, and even less opportunity to control how the other parent behaves. See this as a helpful thing! Giving up the need to control can release an enormous amount of energy, which we can use to stay open to situations and respond helpfully to what happens. In my experience, everyone around me benefits from this too.

Finally, in the words of one Buddhist parent, 'Children refuse to become extensions of our egos, refuse to take our "good" advice, refuse to engage with what we missed out on in life and therefore (well-meaningly) offer to them. They refuse to tread our little hamster wheel of views and values; they don't want to be our representative on earth beyond our deaths. They grow up and leave and create their own lives.'

As a parent, there are hundreds of opportunities to let go of our expectations of our children, let go of planning their future, and let go of getting it right. Being a parent is an opportunity to look at our expectations, for our children and for ourselves, and how this affects the responses and choices we make. Again, noticing this in relation to our children we can also, at least from time to time, take a step back and look at whether we have similar views or expectations of how other people should be, or a set view of how we think the world should be. If so, maybe we can try to keep bringing this awareness to mind, allowing it gradually to challenge expectations and open us to seeing other people as they are.

buddhist teachings via jake, aged nearly two

During a particularly challenging period when her son was nearly two years old, a friend of mine used to describe her young son as 'dissatisfaction on legs'. If anyone was eating, he wanted what they were eating, and he screamed and screamed if he didn't get it, even if it was something he didn't like. He could go through his entire day that way, distressed by not getting what he wanted, which was generally whatever other people had. If he was given that for which he was screaming, it often made things worse because he didn't like it – which was why he hadn't been given it in the first place! Even if he succeeded in getting what he wanted, and he liked it, his satisfaction was momentary. He would then notice his sister and want whatever she had or what she was doing, with further rage and upset when it wasn't immediately handed over or proved to be unsatisfactory.

What Jake was so ably acting out is a good illustration of what are called in Buddhism the four noble truths, and he offers some insight into what they mean. This is an early and fundamental teaching of the Buddha, associated with impermanence, in which the Buddha said that (1) suffering exists, (2) there is a cause of suffering, (3) suffering can be ended, and (4) there is a way to end suffering.

The first truth – that suffering exists – is evident and audible with Jake. During that mercifully short phase of his life, he was undeniably suffering a great deal of the time, despite his secure home and loving family. It is easy for even the untrained observer to identify the cause of his suffering, the second noble truth. It is not difficult to see that Jake was largely creating his own frustration, pain, and dissatisfaction by constantly wanting things that were not available to him, did not satisfy him, or at best provided momentary satisfaction. You may also be able to see that there could be an apparently simple end to Jake's suffering, if he would only realize it. If he would only stop craving things that could not bring him satisfaction, and learn to be happy with the toys and people around him, he would, magically and instantly, no longer suffer, at least for a while. The fourth noble truth is that there is a way to end suffering. In traditional Buddhism, that way is called the noble eightfold path,[7] one of several formulations or descriptions of the path to Enlightenment, the different stages of which are largely covered within this book. However, for Jake it initially meant getting over being nearly two years old and mastering the skill of speech.

So that describes the suffering of a nearly-two-year-old, but what has that got to do with us, unless we happen to be living with such a two-year-old? Maybe nothing in the description of how Jake went about his life in that phase resonates with how you live or how you see others around you living. Or perhaps there is an inkling of recognition. What I find most powerful about the four noble truths is the teaching that it is not the world and life per se that causes us grief, but how we respond to what does and doesn't come our way. Key within this is our response to people, experiences, objects, emotions, moments in time, and so much more, as if they were substantial or in some way capable of providing us with lasting satisfaction. But they are not. Nothing is. Because everything, including us, is subject to change. Buddhism teaches us that – precisely because everything changes and is dependent on other things – it has no fixed, unchanging aspect. Nothing that is conditioned in this way can bring us lasting satisfaction, because everything in the world is insubstantial.

Children can be great teachers, reminding us over and over again what this truth means, giving us the possibility of understanding it on deeper levels, and changing the way we respond. By watching children, we can see how nothing is ultimately satisfying, and this can lead to insight both into our self and the wider reality of what is to be human.

Complex strategic computer games used to keep my son absorbed for months, but each eventually lost its appeal. You may also notice that older children can spend a lot of time anticipating an event or possession of something they believe will bring great happiness, then often – though not always – be slightly disappointed by the reality when it comes around, or it does not hold their attention for long before they want the next thing. You might notice that you have those experiences yourself.

How different are children's responses from ours, really? Is life so different for us, or are we simply more civilized and controlled in our responses? Do we have the same difficulty finding satisfaction and a more peaceful, expansive way of being? How much of our waking lives are spent wanting something or anticipating what is to come, only to find a vague sense of dissatisfaction when it arrives?

Maybe you feel quite happy a lot of the time, or you certainly don't recognize an active sense of suffering. 'Suffering' is quite an extreme word. You might be more familiar with an underlying or intermittent sense of dissatisfaction or discomfort, feeling at times restless, bored, or unsettled, or feeling that you don't belong, you don't quite fit in, or a sense of an empty space in your heart that is not being filled, something missing or not quite right, or just beyond our reach. The Buddha described the suffering he saw as akin to the discomfort that arises when things don't fit or work properly together, the jarring quality we can experience in the course of our everyday life, like the discomfort of 'an ill-fitting chariot wheel' – a warped bicycle wheel might be a more up-to-date analogy. I find this most noticeable when I arrive somewhere I want to be, but I can't settle, a sense that I would be happier sitting over there than over here, but after I move the feeling doesn't go away. It is precisely this feeling of dissatisfaction, restlessness, and boredom that can also be a gateway to the spiritual life, to the realization that there must be more to life, and the search for a different way of being in the world.

Or we could have a baby. In our society there seems to be a widely held belief that if anything is ultimately satisfying, it is having children, as though this can make us whole or complete, fulfilling life's purpose. I have certainly heard, from those unable to have children, the strong sense that only a child can fill that yearning and make them more complete. My heart goes out to people in that situation. I continue to find being a parent deeply satisfying and a source of joy on a great many levels. However, herein also lies one of the pitfalls of parenting when it comes to the spiritual path.

Raising children does appear to give my life much meaning and purpose and make me less likely to ask questions about why I am here than I might otherwise. Becoming parents, our responses to our children, and our absorption in their lives, can mask the inherent unsatisfactoriness of which the Buddha spoke, which can be a way in to the spiritual life. While raising children can open us to a world of constant change, enabling us to be alive to that reality, at the same time there is a danger that having children can delay or prevent us from asking deeper questions, or experiencing this inherent unsatisfactoriness, and therefore from the spur to look beyond our everyday lives. It did not happen to me, and I doubt you would be reading this book if it had happened to you, but it might be helpful to be aware of the possible danger of narrowing our focus to seek complete satisfaction through an exclusive focus on the immediate family and overlooking a possible spur to spiritual inquiry. Indeed, it could also be said that relying primarily on children for satisfaction could lead to our placing unrealistic expectations on them or making it harder to let them go.

The way I see it, having babies and raising children is a major part of the context in which I am living my life, at least for a twenty-year period or so. After that, I sincerely hope I will still be a parent, but that will be relegated to a less central part of my life. Either way, parenting is not the purpose or meaning of my life. What is central is the aspiration to move towards Enlightenment. This I see as the most helpful and positive aspiration I can have, for me, those around me, and any positive influence I can have in the world. Within the context of that aspiration, what is crucially important is *how* I live my life, including being a parent.

Because we do have the capacity to change how we respond to life, there is a way to end suffering, that is, by changing how we live our lives and how we respond to whatever comes our way. We do this because of our aspiration for spiritual growth and through bringing awareness to our lives, in the way described in this and many other books. What we are seeking is a combination of the powerful love and engagement described in earlier chapters, with a felt understanding of and openness to the reality of impermanence. And we need look no further than our children for endless opportunities to open ourselves to the fact that everything changes, and allow that reality to transform us and our responses to life in all its richness.

5

the practice of ethics

When I came to write this chapter, I had to ponder what, from the very extensive Buddhist teachings on ethics, I most wanted to communicate – what was most important to me as a parent, clumsily feeling my way along a spiritual path. I did not have to think for long. What quickly emerged for me were not thoughts but two feelings: a deep sense of gratitude, and a solidity and reassurance born from an ablity to touch base with a welcome clarity.

I am grateful for the accessible, step-by-step approach that Buddhism offers us, that enables us to face, deal with, and move on from those occasions when we have done or said something that weighs on our conscience. This works for day-to-day examples as well as the bigger stuff that can haunt us and suggest we are a bad person. Buddhism offers an effective way to a clearer conscience without letting us off the hook.

The sense of solidity and clarity I feel relates to the five precepts – training principles in ethical behaviour. We saw in the previous chapter that the constant flow of cause and effect is central to Buddhism. When applied to how we behave in the world, this becomes 'actions have consequences'; everything we say and do has an effect. I find this liberating and empowering in many ways, because it helps give me confidence that even though choices and small actions might appear to have no effect in the larger scheme of things – such as environmental actions or moments of patience with our children – they all have an effect at some level. The precepts offer a framework for how to behave and respond to whatever arises, so that the consequences will be as positive as possible. The precepts can also be extremely useful in grounding us when faced with dilemmas or difficult choices. They help me to respond to tales of what is going on in the playground, for example, and in trying to teach my children positive ways to respond to whatever they encounter in the outside world.

the way to a clear conscience

One of the larger loads I have carried on my conscience and then left by the wayside is the fact that my children do not live with both their parents. I felt a lot of emotions after I ended my marriage, and one of them was guilt. I remember telling my father this when he came to see me soon after the separation was agreed. We went out for a meal to talk about what had happened. A lifelong Catholic, he almost exploded, 'Pah, unhelpful Catholic stuff, guilt, you don't want to be doing with that!' I still smile and feel huge waves of love for him when I remember that conversation, and it did help me start to let go of the feeling.

However, several years later I realized that what was driving me to work so much, sleep so little, and try so hard to compensate for my children only having one parent at a time was guilt, at least partly. Having to pay a mortgage on my own also contributed. There was a hitherto unconscious voice saying something along the lines of, 'Yes, I ended the marriage, but at least I am suffering for it,' – a voice fuelled by some long-gone and unhelpful view lodged in my subconscious. I was driving myself too hard. It was not kind, it was not doing me any good, and my exhaustion meant I was often irritable, which wasn't much fun for my children or anyone else. That was the point at which I realized I had to forgive myself, let go, and move on. No one else could give me permission to do that and there was nothing external that was going to release me from that cycle. So I did.

1 – be clear what you have done

First, I unpicked and clarified what I had and had not done 'wrong', where there was and was not something I regretted doing and might be a source of remorse. I was satisfied that I got married in good faith, with the right intentions, and also that remaining married would not have been positive or helpful for anyone involved. I came out of the process certain that ending my marriage did not run counter to the precepts.

Clarity is the first step in this approach. If you apply this to something that is weighing on you, you may find it is immediately obvious what you have done or said that you regret – or not. It is not always possible to avoid upsetting others, and this is particularly true when raising children. We are bound to deny them something they want, or prevent them behaving in ways that might seem great fun to them at the time. If someone is cross with you, it doesn't necessarily mean you have been unskilful or unkind. Buddhism teaches us that it is our state of mind that counts. Check out your intention or motivation. This is the basis from which we can assess what we have done or said. If you are still unsure, you could talk with a friend and ask them to help you clarify what it is you feel uncomfortable about. I did that when going through this process of clarification in relation to ending my marriage.

During this process of clarification, one thing I did was disentangle pain from blame and guilt. This is really valuable in many situations, and something we might not do enough. Prevalent ways of thinking increasingly encourage us to believe that if someone is in pain, whether physical, mental, or emotional, there must be someone to blame, even to sue for compensation. Not only is that always far from true, it is also a distraction from the process of trying to clarify, deal with, and move on from what has actually happened and the feelings and emotions involved.

My separation from my ex-husband was, and is, painful –
my children would rather live with both their parents,
their father misses out on a lot, and life as a single mum is
tough at times. It was really tough at first. At the same time,
I don't believe there is any blame or guilt. That has allowed
me to acknowledge and accept the pain, stop trying to
overcompensate, and stop blaming myself or mentally
beating myself up. That has definitely lightened the load.
From this space I am free to make the best of the context we
have. My ex-husband has decided how much time he
spends with our children, Jai and Ella have a good life,
secure in the love of both their parents, and I thoroughly
appreciate the child-free time this opens up.

2 – allow yourself to feel remorse

Despite this clarity about ending my marriage, there was
still an underlying discomfort that affected how I felt and
behaved. During one particular meditation retreat, I sat for
ages with horrible sick feelings about the fact that my children's father is now absent and part-time, that he did not
chose this relationship with his children, and all he misses
out on as a result. I recognized this uncomfortable churning as remorse, and consciously brought my attention to
the physical feeling as gently and kindly as I could. Despite
my urge to excuse myself, rationalize it, come up with justifications or blame, or run away, I took my awareness to the
physical feelings in my body, and gave them more attention than the thoughts, as the latter seemed to alternate
rather unhelpfully between trying to let me off the hook
completely, telling me I was horrible, or reminding me of
the delinquency that often befalls children from broken
homes.

Remorse is seen in Buddhism as a very positive emotion. It
is not easy to feel. It is physically uncomfortable, either
somewhat humiliating or actively painful, depending on
what it relates to. In my experience, remorse tends to feel

uncomfortable and not something I want to sit with at all, including the humiliation I described above in relation to Jai's tantrums. According to Buddhism, remorse is positive when we have done something unskilful and is essential in order to move on. That is often my experience. The feelings will shift if you choose to give them attention and encouragement, especially if you stay with the physical sensations rather than thoughts such as rewriting what happened, what you should have done, justifications, and the rest. You don't need to stay with the physical sensations for long. They will usually shift and give rise to a desire to move on. They may also enable you to address what you have done or said, combined with a desire to take action.

Remorse is very different from guilt. Buddhism is very clear on the subject of guilt: it is unhelpful. Inherent within it is an aspect of mental and emotional self-flagellation that is simply unkind. 'Guilty feet have got no rhythm' is a song line that may be familiar to some of you, and in our spiritual lives we want to be able to dance – free, happy, open, and with a clear conscience. Guilty feet will drag heavily on the spiritual path. Of course, you can't necessarily stop feeling guilty at will. 'Oh, guilt – that's not helpful, I'd better stop,' tends not work on its own. At worst, it can add another layer of guilt as we beat ourselves up for feeling such an unhelpful emotion. We have an extraordinary capacity to tie ourselves in such knots.

Like any shift in habitual responses, it takes practice and awareness for this to change. However, the process of staying with physical sensations that arise in relation to what we have done or said, rather than follow mental storylines, really is effective. Try it for yourself, if you haven't already. You can see for yourself the extent to which guilt is an endless mental loop, whereas physical sensations of remorse open a doorway to do something about it, move on, and lighten your conscience, making you happier.

3 – make amends, apologize, confess

Out of the churning feelings of remorse came a strong desire to apologize to my ex-husband that the end of our marriage had such an effect on his life and his relationship with our children. I eventually did this in a letter, though admittedly later than I had intended. Arising from feelings of remorse, you may find you do have a desire to set things straight. This is not always possible but, if it is, I would urge you to do it, though you might need to think carefully or talk through the best way to do it to avoid unnecessary pain. That which enables us to move on may or may not involve those affected by our original actions.

Many parents I talked to said they made a point of apologizing to their children if they had reacted in ways they regretted, and this is certainly something I do, particularly when I have been inconsistent because of tiredness, distraction, or stress. Buddhism has a tradition of confession to trusted friends, which can help to shift things, especially when you don't have the option to apologize or make amends directly. All a friend needs to do is listen to you, and preferably acknowledge what you say with a simple phrase such as, 'I hear and accept your confession.'

Although I have never hit my children, I occasionally used force to restrain Jai when he was younger, sometimes squeezing his arm or slightly shaking him. I always felt dreadful afterwards. On retreats, I twice made a resolution never ever again to touch my children in anger. I would offer this to the shrine as a written resolution, or just say the words in my head, too ashamed to say it out loud. The first resolution did not stop me immediately, but there were only one or two more occasions. After the second, that was it. Making a conscious, ritual resolution added the extra awareness and resolve I needed, and I would highly recommend it, whether you do it in private or with friends. Ritual can be very powerful in this way. Even if it is not appropriate to make a resolution for the future, there may be another form of ritual that makes sense to you. I have also done rituals when other past actions have surfaced.

4 – forgive yourself
It wasn't until I wrote this chapter that I found I really had forgiven myself for the fact my children and their father don't live together. I never consciously went through a process of forgiveness, but I am aware that those forces that pushed me so hard are no longer there and I feel very open when talking with Jai and Ella about how it has been for them. After going through the process of clarification, remorse, and apology, it's possible that writing about it has also had an effect. In fact, letting go of that load has shifted a number of things, and made some boundaries clearer.

As parents, we probably get plenty of practice in forgiving our children. If they do something unkind, you probably find a way to forgive them and move on. You might understand that they are growing up and learning how to be themselves, and they are entitled to make mistakes. So are we. We are also growing and trying new things, and discovering the consequences. We are also learning, and this takes time. Our responses are common human experiences. Stumbling is inevitable, so we can try to bring the same compassion, understanding, and unconditional love to ourselves, our humanness, and our spiritual growth, and treat ourselves as we treat our children. You know from forgiving your children that you have the capacity to forgive. We need to bring that capacity to ourselves as well.

happiness, openness, and clarity
Bring to mind something uncomfortable you have done or said, and notice how it feels in your mind or body. Maybe it weighs you down a bit. Perhaps start with something relatively minor, like snapping at someone because you were tired or irritable. Turn your attention to the feelings in your

body or the thoughts in your mind. You may find some tightness, little niggles about small things, or pain associated with more significant acts. Then bring to mind something positive you have done or said to someone. Think back to a generous act or rejoicing in someone, or clearing up a misunderstanding, apologizing, or forgiving someone. Again, focus your attention on bodily feelings, maybe your heart area or stomach, and then your mind. You may find happier or lighter feelings.

You can easily see for yourself how ethical behaviour is linked to happiness and to spiritual growth. The desire for happiness is something all human beings have in common. It is a thread that connects us and drives us to do what we do and make the choices we make. Accounts of the life of the Buddha and his followers make it clear that they were very happy people. Such was evident to those who met them, many of whom asked for teachings because they, too, wanted to be happier. Ethical behaviour and happiness are closely linked. How can we skip lightly along a spiritual path if we are weighed down by our past actions? Imagine how it would feel to have a completely clear conscience. The image I have is one of lightness, almost a bubbliness, in my heart and mind, of being more able to skip and dance. I want this! By going through this process in relation to my past actions, I find I feel more open, more solid, less fearful, without the need to keep dodging or suppressing the consequences of what I have done or said.

It has often been during meditation, particularly on retreat, that my past actions have surfaced from forgotten depths and found some form of resolution to release me from their weight, as with the end of my marriage. Bouts of things have come up over many years, and I keep thinking I must be getting near the end of clearing out the gunk. The more open and aware we become, the more things seems to bubble to the surface, having bided their time until we are able to deal with them properly. It has not stopped, but if what bubbles up is more subtle, I take that as a good sign that the heaviest issues have already surfaced and been dealt with and released. Similarly, if I have recently done something that goes against how I am trying to live, it sits with me in meditation and takes up the space. It quickly becomes obvious that I need to do something about it. None of this is very comfortable, and it is often unwelcome at the time. However, as the Buddha said, without ethics, there is no meditation and no wisdom; things we feel uncomfortable about just have a habit of popping up and getting in the way of openness and clarity in meditation.

This is why I feel such gratitude for what Buddhism offers us in this area – a way to move on in four (not so) easy steps. You needn't be weighed down by what you have done. You can go through the steps above in the space of a minute, after saying something you regret, for example. We can all have a clear conscience. A completely clear conscience may be a long-term vision, but our load will get lighter as we go and we will get better at it. The process is powerful and effective. It does lead to a lightening and clearing of the conscience, which is essential for happiness and spiritual growth. Remorse can return of course, even after apologies, confession, or attempts to repair damage, but they usually do so with diminishing power each time. So remember, we all have access to this – if sometimes uncomfortable – way to move on without letting ourselves off the hook.

In brief, (1) be clear what you have done, (2) allow yourself to experience feelings of remorse, (3) make amends, apologize, or confess, and (4) forgive yourself.

the buddhist precepts
The clarity of the Buddhist precepts is the other aspect of Buddhist ethics I enormously appreciate, because they enable me to touch base with very clear guidelines when things get complicated. For example, one father I interviewed said, 'I have to think continually how to deal with

things. For example, my son now plays with water pistols and I have to sort out what I think about that. I got all this stuff sorted out in my late teens. Now I have to think it through again. Dealing with my son has made me less dog-matic. When dealing with someone whose personality is being formed day by day, there are more shades of grey than I thought.'

We may feel we are clear on certain issues, but then be directly challenged to explain ourselves to our teenagers, or find we are suddenly questioning ourselves about some of the choices we make for our younger children. This all helps us to keep our beliefs fresh, alive, and meaningful, and the precepts can be a cornerstone in this process. There are a number of lists of Buddhist precepts, of which the five precepts is the best known. They are described as training principles rather than rules, and indicate the way an Enlightened person would naturally behave. In the remainder of this chapter, I will draw on the experience of various parents to explore some of the ways I appreciate their clarity and how they can help us live and grow while raising children. There are doubtless many other ways in which they are relevant. The five precepts are,

I undertake to abstain from taking life.
With deeds of loving-kindness I purify my body.

I undertake to abstain from taking the not-given.
With open-handed generosity I purify my body.

I undertake to abstain from sexual misconduct.
With stillness, simplicity, and contentment
I purify my body.

I undertake to abstain from false speech.
With truthful communication I purify my speech.

I undertake to abstain from taking intoxicants.
With mindfulness clear and radiant
I purify my mind.

deeds of loving-kindness

One evening, when my daughter screamed right into my face after no more provocation than a light 'nearly bed-time', my instant response was to reach out and hug her and tell her I loved her. She melted and went quietly to bed. My partner later pointed out that it was rare to see anger met by love and the power that can have. Yet it was easy for me to do. All I saw was a very tired child in need of calming, love, and sleep. The words she screamed had no effect, and I was later able to talk to her, calmed and more receptive, to point out that screaming at people is unkind and unacceptable. This was easy for me, but it was also helpful to have fed back to me what had happened – that this was the positive form of the first precept in action, a small and easy deed of loving-kindness, and that the consequences were positive.

The ability to respond with love is a gift, even if we don't always have access to it. With children, we can often see immediately and repeatedly how our anger or our love has an effect. This can help reinforce our choices and encourage us to respond more often from a basis of love, because we can see it works and is helpful, that it has more positive consequences than anger. Having that bedtime moment fed back to me helped to remind me of this when I didn't feel so calm or spacious and might have otherwise screamed back. The memory of such moments can remind me to take in how someone is, rather than rush to take things personally or react to what they say, and that includes responding to people outside my family. A response based on love works with adults too.

The negative form of this precept – not taking life – sounds cut-and-dried and easy to follow, but it too has many implications. I will stop my children's friends if I find them stamping on insects they consider ugly or scary. At primary school, Jai and one of his friends went through a stage of

99

trying to protect small creatures from such treatment. It did not win them many friends, but this small example illustrates the clarity and principle behind this precept – the principle of not taking life holds true regardless of size, intellect, or apparent ugliness.

Jai has always been fascinated by insects, and even when collecting them as temporary pets, he would ensure they had a comfortable place in a box, and usually managed to release them before they died in captivity. However, despite his general readiness to protect and care rather than kill (except on screen, where he does loads of killing), Jai was furious with my decision on one occasion. We had gone to Chile to celebrate my father's seventieth birthday at his father's birthplace. This was a trip that we were very lucky to be able to do, and it has stayed with us for a great many reasons. While looking around the stalls by the beach, Jai found a beautifully engraved ornamental sword and desperately wanted to buy it. I suspected it was made from the bill of a swordfish, so I said no. Jai pushed, so I asked the stallholder. It had been made from a swordfish that had been hunted and killed to make such ornaments, as well as for their meat. Jai insisted; the swordfish was already dead! I pointed out that more swordfish would be killed to replace every sword bought by tourists.

As far as I was concerned, the issue was completely clear-cut according to the first precept. I was on solid ground and it was easy for me to stay calm and not be swayed by the barrage of arguments. We do need to know what we think is right until our children are old enough to know for themselves. Maybe they then need a bit more rope to work it out for themselves. Being clear about our choices and our boundaries can keep us calm when our views are challenged, and I need that. Jai is clever, persuasive, and knows me very well. I still laugh at myself when I remember a conversation in a shop when Jai tried to persuade me to let him buy a particular computer game about cowboys and

Indians killing each other. 'But it's about cooperation. You have allies and you find ways to work together to help each other,' he said. He knew that would fit better with my values and it did. We bought the game.

I haven't questioned my decision to be a vegetarian for nearly two decades now, because it is integral to the principle of not taking life. However, I was vegetarian before I encountered Buddhism, so this has not required any significant effort. My shift to vegetarianism was accelerated after my parents moved to the countryside and, inspired by the television series *The Good Life*, decided to produce, in addition to home-grown vegtables, their own free-range eggs. They bought six yellow fluffy ducklings from our farming neighbours, which I helped to raise. They looked very sweet waddling about the lawn. Unfortunately, five turned out to be drakes. In a valiant attempt to avoid sentimentality and stand by their self-sufficiency, my father and uncle killed four of them and we ate them at a festive meal.

It's not easy to kill a duck. They have very strong necks. My father and uncle both looked rather pale and sick afterwards and I don't think anyone enjoyed them very much, though none of us dared say so, except perhaps my younger sister who was better than me at voicing things. We never risked getting any more. After that, I completely gave up meat when I was travelling and working in Latin America in my early twenties. I was once wandering around a Bolivian street market, curious and fascinated, and rounded a corner to find a partially butchered sheep lying on the pavement. That confrontation with another presentation of meat, so much harder to avoid than the cellophane-wrapped packages in supermarkets, was enough to stop me eating it ever again.

Twenty years down the line, my children made me think again about this choice and I found it uncomfortable. My son went through a particularly rapid preadolescent growth spurt and frequently became ill. I was told he needed more protein, so I bought neat packages of chicken breast and sliced and cooked them for him. Around the same time, constant pleading wore down my resistance to acquiring two kittens. Then someone asked what I would feed them; I simply hadn't thought about it. Vegetarian cat food is available, but apparently it does not go down very well with them. I started to wonder whether feeding meat to others was really any different from eating it myself, and what was the basis of my vegetarianism if the principle did not hold when pushed. We ended up with two kittens who add a welcome playfulness to the household, I stopped cooking chicken, and Jai continued to grow and to love and nurture his kitten. My children keep issues alive for me, cutting through my easy complacency and keeping me thinking about the ethics of the choices I make.

In its negative form, the first precept goes far beyond not killing. It enshrines the principle of non-violence: that we should avoid harming living beings in any way. Not doing harm also means ensuring that we fulfil our potential and enable our children to do the same. Once we know what we are capable of, not fulfilling this potential harms ourselves or our children. This includes our own spiritual potential. Seen in this light, finding the space we need to grow spiritually is part of living according to the first precept, as is the kindness that we need to direct towards ourselves over and over again when tiredness, distraction, and irritation take over and we behave in ways we are trying to avoid.

not taking the not-given

After the tsunami, we stayed on in Sri Lanka, going inland for a few days before returning to the coast. Before we left, we bought quite a few souvenirs and gifts for friends and family, not least because of the almost complete lack of tourists. Many people who made their living from tourism had lost their means of livelihood. On our last full day, Jai and Ella went to their favourite shop to spend the last of their pocket money, and Ella came out delighted with a tiny ornament which she proudly showed me. I gently broke it to her that it was made of coral. She immediately started crying and was obviously very distressed, until I pointed out that she could take it back to the shop and choose something else instead. I thought she might feel too shy or self-conscious or find it difficult to part with, but she didn't hesitate. I felt very proud of her.

Not taking the 'not-given' is more comprehensive than not stealing, and I find it very helpful in its clarity. This precept extends to not taking more of the earth's natural resources than can be replenished, more than is freely shared and renewed. I didn't know Ella knew anything about coral; how fragile the reefs are and how long it takes them to grow. But she did know, and she didn't want to feel responsible for something that should not have been taken from the sea in the first place, something not freely given. Taking it back to the shop and explaining why will also have an effect at another level. Our actions have consequences for the environment, so ethics can also be about honouring our connection with other people and with the earth. One reason to try to follow the precepts and live ethically is to leave positive, helpful footprints behind us as we go through life.

How do you feel about tax calculations or being given too much change in a supermarket? Taking the 'not-given' also includes how we relate to the state, institutions, and commercial businesses, and taking up people's time and energy without ascertaining whether they are willing to give it. You can try to identify cutting edges for yourself, or grey areas within your family and beyond, to explore for yourself what this really means. The Buddhist system of ethics is all about us: our intentions and what we do. What we take, and from whom, is completely irrelevant.

Within this, it is also important to be aware of the need for generosity towards ourselves, particularly with babies or young children who will naturally demand and take what they want without much regard for whether our time and energy is freely given. We need to take opportunities to give ourselves space and nourishment too. We can also try to open ourselves to receive from other people; receive with open arms whatever is given in that spirit. I often have difficulty receiving in this way. Perhaps it can help to remind ourselves that refusing support, energy, or anything else that is offered is refusing the giver the opportunity to open their hands in an act of generosity.

stillness, simplicity, and contentment

The Buddha made no pronouncements about what is right or wrong; we can be married or single, homosexual or heterosexual, monogamous, polygamous, or celibate and still observe this precept. What is important is that we are careful not to cause harm or unnecessary pain through anything to do with sex. Although it has taken me a long time to live by this precept, I do find this delightfully straightforward in terms of my own life and relationships. I am aware of the example I set my children as they become sexually active. Parenting gives us the ultimate incentive to behave in ways that are positive and helpful. Children learn by imitation, especially when they are young. Whether children repeat or do the opposite of what they see in their parents, they will be strongly affected and influenced by what we say and what we do. What more powerful incentive can there be?

If doubts or uncertainties arise, we can refer back to intention, question whether our actions and choices are based on kindness, and encourage our children to do the same. It is not always possible to avoid causing pain, and we also need to avoid causing harm to ourselves. We can remind ourselves that as human beings we have the capacity for self-awareness, and I find this useful as a message I would like to convey to my children. Sex may be an extremely powerful urge, but we can still be aware of our intentions and what we are doing.

I like the three words used in the positive form of this precept – stillness, simplicity, and contentment – and how each resonates with how I want to live. We all have opportunities to develop stillness, simplicity, and contentment in relation to sex. You could try dropping each into your mind, in the light of this precept, to see what they evoke. Stillness evokes for me a sense of peacefulness and happiness. I find it powerful to remind myself that my children will learn from me by example, and this is a great incentive to live in a way that exemplifies stillness, peacefulness, and happiness. When I drop 'simplicity' into my mind or heart, it does not crowd my mind and take up energy with complications such as affairs or investing energy in wanting what I cannot have, for example. I really do want to keep it simple, so that sex does not take a central place in my life and leaves me free and spacious. And 'contentment': we are aiming to feel contented with our choices and our lot, regardless of how we choose to live and whether or not we are sexually active.

truthful communication

Children provide a fabulous opportunity to be aware of what we say. On the most basic level, it will often be said back to us. If I swear while driving, for example, my children immediately scold me. They constantly pick me up on inconsistencies, particularly if I say things I have told them not to say. In the Pali scriptures, the Buddha is often referred to as the Tathagata, which is sometimes translated as 'one who acts as he speaks and speaks as he acts'. The fact that this constitutes almost a definition of Enlightenment shows how rare a quality complete truthfulness really is. Truthful communication is about integrity, trying to avoid saying one thing in certain company and something else if we are with different people, and about striving for consistency between what we believe and what we say, and between what we say and what we do. This is a gradual process, requiring patience and kindness towards ourselves as we become more aware of what we say.

A parent of teenagers talked to me about conversations with her daughters around the time of a parliamentary election. They talked about climate change, and she often found her children thinking about what was important to them. Her children started questioning why she had a car, which way she voted, and why. She found it quite challenging. As her children homed in on beliefs and behaviour and took issue with her, she found herself asking whether some of the idealism of her younger life had slipped, and whether her behaviour was still consistent with what she claimed to believe. She found this helped her to keep hold of what was important, and she appreciated being kept on her toes and examining her choices. She also enjoyed watching her children engaging with the wider world.

It still makes my heart swell and brings a smile to my face to remember the time when Ella, tiny hands on hips, turned squarely to face me, a rare flame of defiance in her eyes, and announced, 'You can't *make* me go to McDonald's!' It was one of those moments. I had two tired and hungry children and few options about what to get them, and decided to make an exception to my boycott of McDonald's, simply because there was not much else. But Ella wouldn't let me. I had previously told her why we didn't eat at McDonald's, so to her it was simply not right to go against that just because she was hungry. She was right, of course, and my 'I was only thinking of getting chips and a milk shake' sounded hollow and feeble against her certainty and indignation. She had picked me up on my own lack of consistency. I was falling far short of acting as I spoke, or speaking as I acted.

Another example that springs to mind is how we teach children to respond when receiving a gift, presented with love and good intentions, which they don't really want. There are ways to do this with integrity, including thanking the giver for the thought. Truthful communication does not necessarily mean saying exactly what we think regardless of the consequences; it does not mean the whole truth and nothing but the truth in all circumstances. The principle of loving-kindness from the first precept runs through all the other precepts, and is helpful when looking at our intentions and unpicking what to say and what not to say. As a general guideline, if what we want to express is not coming from a basis of kindness, it might be better to remain quiet.

mindfulness clear and radiant

I find one story from the life and teachings of the Buddha particularly endearing because it was given in a bit of a rush and shows a very human side of the Buddha, who must have been hungry at the time. The Buddha was apparently in the middle of his almsround, going from house to house asking for food, when a man interrupted him and asked, somewhat urgently, for a teaching. The Buddha asked him to come back later. This man's name was Bahiya, and he had travelled a very long way to find the Buddha and receive a teaching. He wasn't easily deterred. He asked again, and was again asked to wait. And then insisted that he couldn't wait because he was afraid he would die before he heard the Buddha's teaching. It was a tradition that if someone asked three times, he had to be answered, so the Buddha obliged. However, he gave one of his most succinct teachings, 'In the seen, only the seen. In the heard, only the heard....'[8]

Concise this certainly is. It is also profound, and is one aspect of the clarity of mind those on a spritual path are aiming for. What we see or hear is just that; objects and events are just what they are, no more or less. They aren't

107

complicated and overlaid with stories and reactions. There is plenty working against our seeing things for what they are. Try mentally tuning in to some of the media and advertising and see if you can spot examples in which we are told the complete opposite of this teaching: that chocolate will bring happiness, aftershave makes you attractive, other things bring status, a satisfying sexual relationship, and so on. This is what our children hear constantly, and it cannot but have an effect. There are also many messages about what we should and should not do as the perfect parent, so many opportunities to glance at other parents and feel a stab of inadequacy or pride, envy or superiority.

All this can cloud our minds and prevent us seeing things as they are, and seeing only that, detracting from and obscuring the natural clarity and radiance of our minds. The fifth precept also encourages us to abstain from intoxicants. We can interpret intoxicants very broadly; it includes not only alcohol and drugs that cloud our minds, but everything we are exposed to in the course of our daily lives and the thoughts that arise. Bahiya, we are told, became Enlightened on the spot when he heard this teaching. He was killed soon afterwards, so he had been wise to insist. I find it takes me a lot longer for teachings to sink in at all, let alone so profoundly.

Within all these messages, we also have a wealth of opportunities just to notice the stories in our minds, catch ourselves each time it happens, and, with this awareness, gain more clarity and perspective. Raising children is an excellent context in which to do this, because we can also see the world through our children's eyes, hear some of the less subtle messages directed at them, and think about what this very concise teaching means. When it comes to ethics, Buddhism can help us grow as parents, and parenting can keep us on our toes. Ethics are a basic spiritual practice, something we can be doing all the time, and an accessible way to practise spiritually within the context of family life.

6

being alive

Having just returned from a Buddhist meditation retreat, I sat at the kitchen table with Jai one day as he talked enthusiastically about a story he had written and how he wanted to be a writer and poet when he grew up. I felt completely calm and clear-headed, and sheer joy permeated my body. Of course, it was nice to be able to listen to such creative aspirations, a welcome change from a commentary about the latest computer game, but the main difference from my usual experience was that I had just spent a week practising bringing all of myself into the present moment and doing so with an open heart. The usual bedtime distractions of wanting to get him and Ella quickly to bed so that I had some space, or worrying about the work I had to do before I could go to bed, simply did not exist. I was just sitting there with him, one hundred percent present, and entirely happy. I had a deep sense that I wanted nothing else than that moment, that I could die, there and then, feeling complete and fulfilled.

That physical sensation of spaciousness, happiness, and calm arises naturally when we are fully present in the moment. It is not mysterious, and that experience was not uniquely mine; it is accessible to anyone at any moment, wherever we are. Buddhism tells us this is our natural state. Yet, as we all know, to be fully present in the here and now is not easy. You, too, have probably had moments of insight into the spaciousness and intensity that comes with being fully present, and know how that can transform your experience. Yet our minds throw up almost any distraction they can. At that moment with Jai I rather naively thought I had cracked it, that I had brought home what I had learned and experienced on retreat, and I could live like that all the time, entirely present in each moment, experiencing life with intensity and beautifully connected with and appreciative of my children as a result. But the moment passed and such experiences now prove elusive, as they have many times before and since.

The word 'Buddha' means 'one who is awake'. The experience of Enlightenment has been likened to waking up from a dream. One of its features, I am told, is to be fully present, connected, and open to all life, aware of ourselves and what is happening around us. It is not difficult to see that this is different from how we spend much of our lives – anywhere other than in the here and now and, to some extent, insulated or removed from the reality of life around us. We can even do this on purpose, shutting out aspects of the world we don't want because they are too painful or not what we had planned, or almost sleepwalking through our daily routines. After all, who aspires to be fully alive to the washing up or the nappy changing?

Unfortunately we cannot disconnect selectively. We might try to shut out the endless chatter or questioning from young children, and then we wonder why we can't shake ourselves awake and fully present in a long-awaited conversation with a friend, why there is still part of us that is not open to the beauty around us or insists in wandering away somewhere else. As we saw earlier, we can't desensitize ourselves to the bits we don't like and remain fully alive and in touch with what we do want to experience. It just doesn't work like that, not in the long term.

So the essence of Buddhism is to awake, become more alive, and gradually open, to be as present as we can, as often as possible, to resist the temptation to insulate ourselves, to practise being where we are. This takes time and

practice, but the experience of becoming a parent and raising children offers endless opportunities to do just that, to
open us to a level of connection with other human beings
and place us squarely within life, whether we like it or not.
Of course, we can always run away screaming or find new
ways to shut out the new threats and unsavoury features of
life that have appeared. But Buddhism can help us understand, value, and use our experiences as opportunities to
connect more fully and see ourselves within a wider context, chipping away at our habitual tendency to separate
ourselves.

being present in the here and now
A friend told me about something that happened when she
took her young son to the London Aquarium. They hadn't
been there very long before they came to the big shark
tank, a centrepiece that extends up through several levels.
Her son loved it, became completely absorbed, and just
wanted to stay there. She found herself fighting with impatience, wanting to continue the tour as she had planned,
aware of all the other things there were to see. Oblivious of
what was still to come, her son was just naturally present
with the sharks. In the end, my friend caught herself and
saw how she was resisting being in the moment. She
relaxed, let go of her plans, and found it wonderful just
watching the sharks with her son. It transformed her
experience of that outing. Later, she drew on that incident
when she felt bored or frustrated and wanted to move on.
You can probably draw on similar experiences of your
own, or consciously choose to stop and relax with your
children and see if your experience of the moment
changes. This is an area in which our children really can be
our teachers.

It is natural to be that present, yet so many of our human
tendencies, of how we are hard-wired and conditioned,
work against us just being where we are with what we are

doing. There is an objective reality too. As parents, our job includes keeping the structure of family life together, and that can mean planning ahead and generally be in organizing mode. Yet how much of this is entirely necessary? How much is repetition? Can we just make a plan, then relax and be where we are instead? One thing I have found, especially when responsible for several young children, is that even if they are enjoying what they are doing, it is sensible to have a plan for what to do next. Yet I have a choice: I can keep my focus and energy absorbed in planning the next activity, constantly repeating and checking my plans, anticipating the point at which I will have to implement it, or I can simply make a plan, put it to one side, and get on with enjoying the present moment, especially if things are going well and I am not needed; I can relax for a while.

Have you ever had the experience of collecting a young child, asking what they have been doing, only to be told, 'I don't know', 'playing', or 'nothing'? It doesn't seem to be so natural for young children to think back or project their minds forward. This can be quite refreshing, if a bit frustrating. However, it can also act as a prompt or reminder to draw our attention to how much time we spend trying to talk or think about the past or the future.

For years, the constant balancing involved in holding children and performing other tasks at the same time also gave me ample opportunities to keep my mind fully absorbed, anywhere other than here and now. Even if I was trying to meditate, my thoughts ran along the lines of 'If Ella goes to play with Sophie on Thursday and Jai to wherever, then I can go to that meeting and have them back to play the following Tuesday.' And so it went on. Anxiety often accompanied such thoughts. Again, there was a choice. I could choose simply to notice the thoughts and anxieties and decide not to follow them. There is no need either to push away thoughts and emotions or get involved in the detail and follow them. You can just note there is a puzzle that you can solve some other time, and bring yourself back to whatever you had chosen to do.

Unfortunately, I don't believe there is a short cut to being more present with where we are and what we are doing, or not one we can rely on encountering. However, we can develop that ability quite simply through practice. One analogy I find particularly helpful is that of developing muscles. The only way to strengthen and maintain biceps, for example, is by flexing them, repeatedly and regularly. It is the same with becoming more present to our experience. Every time we notice our attention is elsewhere, or lost in stories, we can simply notice it and notice where we are, what we are doing, our body and our feelings. Each time you do that, it is like one more flex of those muscles. And the more we do it, the easier it gets. I still constantly have to organize children and work, but somehow the thoughts revolving around them are not always so close, press in on me less, and leave me more space.

enjoying the journey

One family I spoke to once found there was a building site between their holiday hotel and the beach. Every day, on their way to the beach, the children stopped for a long time to watch the building site, looking into the hole to see what had changed. They had a choice whether to move their children swiftly on, or to stand and look with them as they enjoyed the hole. This reminds me of some beautiful and well-known words I have on the wall in my kitchen, 'There is no way to happiness, happiness is the way.'

As far as those children were concerned, happiness was the way to the beach as much as the beach itself. They brought all of themselves and their attention to the journey, including the fascinating building site. We have a similar choice: we can feel impatient to get where we are going, or we can learn how to enjoy the way. Inherent within this is learning to discriminate less. Rather than label the building site as ugly and the beach as beautiful, we can bring our attention to everything, allow fascination to arise, feel alive, and enjoy whatever crops up along the way. Then we will also be better able to appreciate the beach when we get there, if we ever do.

Etched in my mind is a similar memory of a visit to the shop at the end of our road with Ella. She was a toddler and it was an epic journey for her without a pushchair. I had set out on that particular journey partly to get out of the house and for her to walk, and I was enjoying her erratic progress. As we snailed along, zig-zagging between distractions, someone overtook us and said 'You never get anywhere like that.' She was meaning to be kind and empathize with my slow progress, and I just smiled in response. In my mind were the words, 'There is nowhere to go. This is it. This is what we are doing.' I was content. I was enjoying the journey. At that moment, happiness was the way. That this moment stands out after all these years suggests how often I must be intent on getting to the shop and miss the journey along the way, but even these small moments of happiness along the way can have a big effect on us.

It helps to remind myself that such moments are part of an ongoing spiritual practice, and of my aspiration to be more fully alive to each moment. We are not bringing our attention to where we are because we want to be alive to that experience in particular, and we are not failing if it seems to have no immediate effect. We are doing it because part of our spiritual practice is learning how open to each moment, to give life our full attention, and to live as fully alive and awake as we possibly can. We are not encouraging ourselves to be fully conscious of changing a nappy because we particularly want to sense that smell at that moment, but because we want to sense smells in the whole of our lives and we need to learn how to do so.

being alive

One Buddhist mother who was trying to be more alive to family life told me how she identified individual situations in which she realized she had a strong tendency or temptation to be elsewhere. She described one in particular.

> *I am trying to be in the present more and more. One aspect I am aware of at the moment is that my son likes talking about computer games. I go into mechanical mode, not really listening. I'm engaged in a mechanical way because I find it extremely uninteresting. My view is that computer games are male, that I hate them, and they are not what I'm interested in. But they are part of his life, and the lives of many children today. That is something I've noticed only recently. I do not want to carry on with this response. I don't yet know how to tackle it, but I do have faith that I just need to be conscious of it and it will shift, even though I don't yet know what form that will take.*

It is helpful to identify what events or reactions take us out of ourselves and make us shut off from awareness. If we remain conscious that we want to change this response, we can be more open to practising being present in those situations.

How do you know when you have achieved that greater presence and awareness? You might feel a sense of space, contentment, or enjoyment, or an absence of the frustration or resistance you are used to in those situations. This might be particularly noticeable within something you do not associate with enjoyment – like walking down a street or listening to computer game exploits. I know that when I am more present and aware, colours appear brighter, smells are more vibrant, and I feel a calm sense of contentment, or I become more aware of energy in my body. Basically, I am happier. I also make better choices, I am

115

more agreeable to be around, and generally more helpful. I aspire to live every moment of my life like that.

multitasking with awareness

I fit in a lot each day. I am not sitting around just breathing for much of it at all. It might sound as if I am saying we can only be aware if we move slowly, and do just one thing at a time – but this is not the case at all. I try to be aware of that too, aware of myself multitasking or moving quickly, to keep some perspective. We can still breathe with aware-ness and bring attention to ourselves and our bodies, at the same time as doing things quickly or several things at once. It is not that we should never plan ahead or use our memo-ries. We don't necessarily have to choose between antici-pating what our children will need next and enjoying what is happening now. Of course, when we multitask we can-not give our full attention to one thing, but we can still be present with ourselves and aware of what we are doing.

It is possible to be content and aware of ourselves, of our heart, and to be able to trust ourselves to make positive choices and speak kindly, even when we are busy. We can then make a conscious choice whether to continue to do several things together or take them one at a time. I find it can also help me tap into a sense of humour to be aware of myself when busy. Sometimes I smile at myself and won-der whether it is really necessary, or so important. How much do we really need to hold together?

That is a question I pose rather than answer, as I believe I hold it together more than I really need to through a com-bination of deeply ingrained habit and fear of who I would otherwise be. I definitely do this less than I used to, but I still do it quite a lot. Sometimes I wonder if it would be better to let it all fall apart and be in childlike mode more often, kicking piles of leaves in the park or sharing a child's moments of awe and wonder at the sharks, the holes in the ground, or the distractions in the street, rather than anxiously trying to move on to the next thing on our adult agenda and missing an opportunity to share some delight.

being in touch with life

Several parents I interviewed talked about losing their habitual insulation with the world around them and starting to live life 'in the raw'. They echoed the experience described by one mother, who said, 'Looking back, it felt as if I was in a bubble and the bubble burst when I had my son. Life became more raw. I was somehow more in touch with things.' One father was aware of how much more in touch with life having a child forced him to be. That is the kernel. In his view, it was just so much more real and unavoidable than anything he had done before. For him, too, the fact that his son is the result of sex, born out of passion and love and lack of foresight, was also a very joyful thing and part of this rawness and immediacy. He and his partner had not intended to have a child, but that was not remotely relevant once he was born. One mother remembered feeling she was suddenly orientated around another centre. She said she often felt completely at sea and occasionally landing on a shore and then being swept back, losing control, and being vulnerable. She was also periodically aware of what an amazing experience that was in many ways for someone so used to feeling in control, despite it feeling so raw and uncomfortable for much of the time.

It can help enormously to see this experience of rawness in a wider context, knowing that how we have been catapulted into feeling is part of what we are trying to do on our spiritual path. We are trying to connect more with life. Our children can remove some of what separates us from life in the raw. Through this perspective, perhaps we can resist the temptation to replace the insulation.

The same can be true at home with young children. Family life can pin us down, stop us looking outward, and make us look more inward. This may be particularly true if a substantial part of our self-image has been tied up with a career from which we have to step back for a while, or even from more overtly spiritual activities such as retreats, workshops, and reading. Our spiritual practice is in the home, living life moment by moment. We have the opportunity to appreciate the wordless, to go beyond the theories of spiritual practice, and experience things in themselves. That is the heart of where we are trying to get to. That can be an important lesson in not searching for the treasure – the spiritual answers and experiences – outside of ourselves; a big opportunity not to look for answers out there, but inwards, in the minutiae of our daily lives.

in touch with energy and playfulness

The energy in our house is palpably transformed when the children get home. They bring with them a vibrancy and aliveness that fills the space. I enjoy the peace and quiet when they are not at home, but my heart lifts when they arrive back. Even if they are irritable and I feel a wave of irritation rising in me in reaction, there is a part of me that smiles in wonder at the amount of life that has just entered my day. They often arrive with an urgency to tell me what they have been up to, spread themselves over a surprisingly wide space, and bring an enthusiasm and engagement that I may have lost touch with in their brief absence, running the risk of being just too grown up.

When I was first drafting this chapter, I was also enjoying the energy and lightness brought into our lives by our kittens and their admirable approach to life, expending a huge amount of energy leaping, completely absorbed by play and demonstrating an endless curiosity with the world, then going to sleep. I have stressed to the children how fleeting this phase will be. I feel the same about my children, aware how fleeting is this phase of their lives, keen to appreciate their energy and playfulness. Much of that phase has passed already, and I feel immensely

grateful for the hours I spent absorbed in sand constructions on beaches over the years, the tunnels becoming
more sophisticated as my children grew up, and the romp-
ing play-fights I would have left to their father had he been
here, but which I thoroughly enjoyed, together with the
trampoline and shared craft projects. The older they get,
the more we can share things that I really enjoy as well.

Of course, it does not all feel positive. I am aware that the
kitten's play is an ongoing rehearsal for the killing of small
creatures. And I find it hard to watch the play-fighting
between boys, having to look away to prevent myself hov-
ering with a constant, 'Do be careful, darling, you'll hurt
him.' I can also feel deep frustration at how children often
choose to direct their energy, and how out of touch they
can seem to be with other aspects of life and the wider
world, spending hours locked into computer games, ener-
getically resisting my attempts to interest them in the
world or take them out somewhere. As children get older,
they seem more likely to say there is nothing to do. One of
the biggest challenges I have faced is having increasingly
to remove their access to computers, to allow the jagged-
ness of boredom and angry youthful energy to fill the
space until they find something better to do.

One half term holiday, partly to get away from the computers, I booked us into a 'family activity break' run by the
Youth Hostel Association. All I had to do was get everyone
to the hostel lobby at a designated time, from where a
series of cheerful male role models took us off to teach us
mountain biking, dinghy sailing, rock climbing, and other
activities, all new to me. It was fabulous and I loved it. At
the end of our few days came our last activity – gorge
scrambling. You might know what this is, but I had never
heard of gorge scrambling and was somewhat surprised to
find that the gorge where we were due to scramble had a
river in it. Apparently quite a popular sport, it consists of
scrambling up waterfalls. I found myself wondering who

first thought of doing that. There was a perfectly good and quite attractive path beside the river, so whose idea was it to walk in the water? I was told whoever had the idea had probably done so in the summer, not in a freezing October in Devon.

Etched in my memory of that short holiday are the last moments of that gorge scramble. Much of the time was spent crawling, as the force of the water was too strong for us to stand upright. Jai bounded on ahead and was often ready, hand outstretched, to help me up the difficult parts. And at one point, I found myself crawling over the rocks next to Ella, my hands in the freezing white water rushing underneath me, and it just seemed to be such a funny thing to do that I started giggling. I looked over at Ella and pointed out that I probably hadn't crawled next to her since she learned to walk. She started laughing too and we ended up rather helplessly getting up that last bit. I felt huge waves of gratitude for these people who will play with me and encourage me to play in that way. I doubt very much that I would have been there if it hadn't been for them.

In our spiritual life, we need energy in huge amounts, and we can open to a great deal of energy by spending time playing with children and young people. As you have probably found yourself, it is not easy to transform our experience and grow spiritually. Much of what we need to do is constantly repeat the same small steps of awareness, and doing so may bring us in touch with more pain than bliss. We need energy to keep going, and being around children can be a great reminder of that. Opening up to enjoy their energy, however directed, can be a boost to our own weaker resources and help remind us to stay in touch with a vibrancy, immediacy, and energy for life.

The giggling in that gorge somehow shifted something for me. For years I had one rather helpful underlying storyline in my mind that my life was hard – as a single working mum and all that. I had been undermining that storyline for years, but this just clinched it in some way. It felt as if the last remnants of that unhelpful belief had been replaced with 'my life is fun'. Of course, both are storylines and neither could be true all the time, but children do open the opportunity for more fun, more play, and the release of lots more energy.

shaking off old habits

During the interviews for this book, several people talked about the birth of a first child as a shattering experience. Some talked about falling apart or breaking into pieces, or how their old self fell apart. One mother said she was just finding the pieces again when her son reached three or four years old, but there was part of her that wanted to keep falling apart and rearranging. Although it was raw and uncomfortable, she intuitively sensed that there was also something positive within that falling apart. It seemed positive to break out of how she was used to being in the world.

In order to grow spiritually, we need to go beyond the fixed, limiting version of ourselves. As we saw in Chapter 3, we all have our stories about who we are and who we are not, and this in itself can hinder our growth. There, we looked at the image of a hard outer shell breaking into pieces, and it is precisely that shell that maintains our fixed idea of ourselves, including our resistance to change.

We will change anyway; it is more a matter of *how* and *what* we bring to the process. If we resist the change into which we might be catapulted when we become parents, for example, perhaps unsuspecting and unprepared, despite the months of pregnancy, we may try to put the pieces back together the same way, to recreate ourselves the way we were, aware of the tension inherent in being unable to stay the same, without benefiting from the potential for growth. Yet within this breaking apart, we see gaps opening between the pieces as opportunities for growth and change, opportunities to keep the pieces in flux, providing a flexibility to who we are and helping us accept that remaining as we were is not an option. If we embrace this disorientating falling apart as an opportunity for spiritual growth, that is what it can be.

the preciousness of human life

One particularly hot summer day, with my belly stretched to bursting and longing for the birth of my second child, I received a card from an old friend called Amanda. She had leukaemia and her card told me that she was going downhill and asked me to send her waves of positive energy. She had lived eleven years longer than the doctors predicted after she was diagnosed with leukaemia in her early twenties, and died five months after Ella was born. I remember being glad to have Ella in my arms at the celebration of Amanda's life and very aware of her heart beating next to mine and the precious new life beginning as another ended.

Amanda and I had worked together at a time when I was less comfortable talking about death than I am now – and I am still far from comfortable with it. She once told me that if she were given a choice, she would not choose to live her life without leukaemia. At the time, I found this really hard to understand. She certainly wanted a cure, to get better, and to live longer, but at the same time she appreciated living with the constant awareness of the proximity of death. It meant that she lived and embraced life with an intensity she doubted she would have experienced without that illness. Facing the prospect of her life shortly to come to an end, she left a secure and interesting job and took up clowning, a long-held dream of hers. That was the focus of her life for her last two or three years, and she loved it.

I now understand what she was trying to tell me. Being aware of mortality, of death, can bring us more alive to the preciousness and transience of life, and therefore help us focus on how we want to live, not putting things off, sorting out conflicts, and putting energy into our spiritual practice, providing a sense of urgency, focus, and commitment which enables us to fight off complacency.

I remember being moved and inspired by a man on the radio talking about the intensity with which he heard birdsong, and how he saw colour in his garden more vividly than ever before, having been diagnosed with cancer and given only months to live. He sounded very happy. You have probably heard of similar experiences. Sometimes the death of someone close to us, as well as being extremely painful, can catapult us into greater awareness of the preciousness of human life, realizing that it will not last for ever. It can even be the gateway to a spiritual journey. But we need not wait for such an event to experience the galvanizing effect of death. The reality is that we are all dying. We may hope for many years rather than months, but we are all dying.

As I write, Ella has started sometimes going to school on her own, or with friends, and my mind throws up vivid images of them becoming distracted and stepping into the path of an oncoming car and certain death. We saw above how children keep us alive to the reality of death, if only through our fears and our imagination. This is especially true when they are very young, and again when they start going out on their own. As parents, we naturally think about death, and hold it closer than we otherwise might. So rather than block it out, we might as well use these thoughts positively, to help us engage with the preciousness of life and embrace it in all its intensity to give us the energy, focus, and commitment we need in order to live our lives more fully.

awareness of our interconnectedness

At her daughter's graduation, one mother found herself sitting in a huge auditorium with hundreds of other parents. It reminded her of school performances when her daughters had been very young: the mixture of delight, pride, and excitement of watching her child on stage. However, at that moment, instead of losing herself in nostalgia and intensity, she found herself stepping back from her experience to become aware of all the other parents in the hall all feeling the same as her. This made her think about parenthood, not just her own experience of watching her daughter graduate. She found herself reflecting on how being a parent is so deeply personal and private, yet also common to so many. Billions share that experience today, countless billions have done so before us, and many more will follow. For her, this was a powerful, felt experience, or insight, into our connections with others. Being a parent is not just about us, we are not separate, we all go through the same range of emotions and experiences.

Personally, I find that even the smallest of presentations in the termly assembly makes me cry. That used to be a source of great embarrassment to both me and my children, but we all accept it as inevitable these days. However, the strength of my emotional reaction is a pitfall in itself, at least in keeping me separate and preventing any awareness of others. In my surreptitious eye-mopping, my experience stays as my thing, and I rarely step back to take in other parents and see how we are all sharing similar responses. Yet within parenting, there are many opportunities to be aware of our lack of separateness and the connections we share, starting with our children and extending in widening circles to include other parents, our own parents, and beyond.

Once you have a child, you have to get used to the fact there is another human being who is vulnerable and dependent on you and about whom you care, maybe more deeply than you have ever cared for anyone. This child will be dependent on you for a long time, and that is something you can't block out without huge cost. As parents, our actions will greatly affect our children, and our happiness is caught up in them. In other words, we can clearly see that we are connected. This is perhaps the most immediate and unavoidable experience we can have of our connection with another person, as not completely separate or independent. According to Buddhism, we grow by realizing the connections we have with others at deeper and deeper levels. Being a parent can be a good place to start, seeing how what we do and say has an affect on one other person, and them on us, and moving out from there.

connecting with our own parents

Even immersed in my own weepy response to seeing my children on stage, I have enough perspective to be aware of the fact that both my parents were exactly the same when we were in school plays. One of the lovely things about my father is his tendency to cry when moved, and my mother cried at my Buddhist ordination ceremony, their only opportunity to see me on any sort of stage for several decades. Reflecting on the similarity between our responses and those of our parents can give us a sense of the continuity from generation to generation, and open us to our connection with our parents – at least if you can sit with that sense without getting lost in stories, analysis of their parenting ability, or judgements.

I interviewed a father whose teenage son turned up one day on his doorstep. He had not raised his son after the first couple of years, and told me he was absolutely unprepared and no idea what he was dealing with when he became involved with his son again. Immediately after that first visit, he rang his own mother and said both 'thank you' and 'sorry'. He understood for the first time what it must have been like for his mother when he himself was a teen-ager. He understood how worried she must have been and also how well she had handled him in his teenage years.

Our experiences as parents and our responses to our children can enable us to relate better to our own parents and perhaps see our connection differently. It can also help us to spread awareness of our connections and chip away the illusion that we are separate and independent.

connecting with other parents

Before Ella was born, my work took me periodically to Latin America. On my last visit, I found myself seated on a bamboo floor interviewing a village chief's wife through an interpreter. There were no walls, and the roof was made of leaves. The country was lush and beautiful. I was in the Amazonian region of Colombia, helping to make a short video for a church youth organization about indigenous people being driven from their land. I had already asked this woman about the once-high river on the banks of which their village was built. A new dam had reduced their water supply, and it was now quite a walk to the water's edge, and she described how their lives were changing. When the interview was over, we struggled to find some common ground or make a connection, until I mentioned that I had a child. Then we talked about children.

She was incredulous when I said most people in my country limited themselves to two or three children. She could not understand why, or how it could cost money to raise a child. She had fourteen children herself, and sat there with a child and grandchild of the same age on her lap. But we did have that common experience that enabled us to make a connection, for which I was very grateful. I still have a photo of her in my sitting room to remind me of our common humanity, a connection with people whose lives could easily feel so remote from mine. I was very sad to leave that village for the long journey back to a very different world.

Recognizing that the parent-child relationship is universal is something we may not understand or connect with before we have children, yet it is a very powerful force in the world. It can give us an insight into the connection between ourselves and other parents, and through that a felt sense of our connection with all other beings.

Many years after my trip to Colombia, I interviewed a social worker whose job was to support families with problems. Herself a mother of teenagers, she told me about her experience of working with a woman who, together with her children, had many problems. This mother stood out in her mind because she talked about how she wanted to do the best for her children. They were all in trouble, either with the police or at school, but the fact that she wanted the best for them was something she had in common with her social worker and all other parents. Wanting the best for their children was something that helped the social worker make a connection with her.

Even those who are not parents have had the experience of being parented, or felt the lack of it. Being a parent is an opportunity to realize and have a felt sense of how we are all connected, over and over again. And it is something we need to keep being made aware of, otherwise we can easily lose sight of it. Somehow we are hard-wired to see ourselves as separate, and being able to realize and reflect on this powerful connection is a gateway to growth. This connection with other beings is what is real, and this is emphasized within Buddhism. We are not separate entities all going our independent ways. We are all connected, and the opportunities that parenting presents can give us an insight into what this means, letting it seep in so that it affects how we see things and the choices we make, better able to live in harmony with how things really are and be happy. It can also be a gateway to realizing our effect on those around us and on the world, so that we tread more lightly and more positively.

connecting in widening circles

One friend of mine felt the force of connections we can make with other parents and with what they are experiencing when her daughter was seriously ill. For her, it was an amazing crash course in human beings, families, how people cope with that sort of situation, and the strong connections people make with each other in such an intense situation. Many of the usual barriers were dissolved by the situation, and she felt acutely aware of the connectedness between her immediate family, her wider family, friends, and everyone else in the hospital.

Having a child can also put us in touch with our insignificance in the wider scheme of things, as part of the countless generations who have gone through this process of giving birth, raising children, and sending them out into the world to have children in their turn and raise them. People are born, people die, life goes on. Because we are interconnected, we cannot shut down to the world in pursuit of our own happiness and expect to find it. Seeing our place in the wider flow of generations can give us a glimpse into what that means.

A Buddhist friend and mentor of mine described this very poetically. One's heart is normally asleep, beating only to the sound of its own heartbeat. But our heartbeat is the heartbeat of everything; it is the heartbeat of the universe momentarily captured in this flimsy and whimsical self, momentarily experienced as separate, but actually it is my heartbeat, your heartbeat, the heartbeat of every living being in the universe, captured momentarily. And therefore we think it is 'me' and try to find its own happiness. The awakening heart dissolves these barriers, awakening to the fact that every heartbeat is the same heartbeat. It may beat with a different rhythm but it is the same life-force, and we can live hearing those heartbeats and realizing they are all the same heartbeat, the heartbeat of the universe.

Even the smallest glimpse into this beautiful reality can have a powerful effect on how we respond on so many levels, how we can see the need to honour our connection with the universe in our behaviour. It may seem remote to experience our own heartbeat as that of the life-force of the universe, or even daunting in its implications, but we don't need to see that all at once. We are seeking glimpses into that reality and an imaginative engagement with ourselves as connected. We have the opportunity to start close to home, to see our heartbeat and that of our children beating as part of the same life-force. We can expand from there when we feel most able to do so, in widening circles, or take a moment to pause and reflect when our day-to-day experiences point to this wider reality. In this way, we gradually allow our heart to awaken, experience ourselves as alive, awake, and in touch with life.

7

growth and maturity

One summer I took my children, then aged 9 and 11, on a Buddhist family camping retreat. They had been adamant that they did not want to go. I had been equally adamant that they should. It would be good for them, I wanted to share an important part of my life with them, and anyway they always enjoyed these events once they got there. I packed the car and went to collect them from their father to drive straight to the camping site, as the path of least resistance. They both refused even to come downstairs to greet me, and after we finally got them into the car they complained the whole way there. A few days later, when we had to leave the retreat, I faced the same problem. They were as furious with me for taking them away from the retreat as they had been for my taking them there in the first place. When I recounted this to a friend she laughed heartily and said, 'It's a good thing you're a grown-up!'

Yes, it is a good thing I am a grown-up. I don't always *feel* like a grown-up. I do still want to stamp my feet and proclaim 'it's not fair' from time to time, and sometimes I do, though Jai and Ella just laughed when I complained about their unreasonable behaviour, and told me it was all part of the 'job description'. Maybe it is. Someone once told me after the birth of her second child that if this was a job, she would have handed in her notice in long ago. The terms and conditions were simply unreasonable. But it is not a job in that sense, and handing in our notice is not an option most of us would seriously consider – except perhaps as a distant fantasy in the tougher moments.

Raising children requires us to be pretty grown up – that is the bottom line. We are in there for the long haul. We can't throw our hands in the air and walk out; we need commitment and staying power. It also requires immense patience and means that we often have to let go of things that feel unfair, let go of doing what we want to do, of having our say, or being properly heard and agreed with. We can relish the energy and vibrancy of youth but, at the end of the day, it is probably us who have to bring in a broader perspective when our children's ability to be fully present manifests as a severe lack of wider perspective in the most minor of arguments. We can allow our children to keep us open to our more playful side and learn from them, but at the same time we will either become more mature through being a parent or spend a lot of time stamping our feet in a rather futile manner. That is a choice we have. We also need a level of confidence to make choices for our children and ourselves, often amid abundant and contradictory messages about what is right and wrong, and how to be a 'good parent' raising happy and well-balanced children.

Fortunately maturity, commitment, patience, and confidence are also extremely handy when it comes to treading a spiritual path. Without them we would soon flounder. Maybe what a spiritual path can best offer within the subject of this chapter is reassurance and encouragement that – however painful this enforced growing-up process can be – it is enabling us to grow as our children grow. Buddhism can offer a bigger picture and a broader perspective as, for example, you reach out to provide for your child's needs yet again when all you want to do is to curl up and be cared for. Seeing this act from a broader perspective can give us an insight into our capacity to commit and follow through, and to stick with things that are not easy. If you allow yourself to recognize this, even marvel at it, it can also build your confidence to follow through on a spiritual path, not throw your hands in the air part way through and give up just because it is tough or you have not managed to live up to your aspirations that day, or even that month.

a sense of perspective

When Jai started secondary school, he seemed suddenly to grow out of all the things he liked doing and that we did as a family. Pretty soon he wanted to spend his whole non-school life on the computer, leaving it only to watch television or play on his Playstation. This tapped into some of my most reactive corners and, with my nose pressed against the glass and a little perspective, my mind had a field-day magnifying the situation until I was struggling with guilt at making computers, televisions, and game consoles too readily available, frustration at the waste of time, fear of how my children – and by inference, the youth of today – would turn out, inadequacy at not communicating a more profound meaning to life, and, most of all, a deep sense of powerlessness. I didn't know what else he liked doing, so I couldn't change the situation. I became critical. Jai decided I was against him and we locked horns: critical mother and sullen preadolescent. Not a lot of fun for anyone.

Then one day, without warning, I momentarily stepped back and glimpsed myself and saw with humiliating clarity what I was doing. I realized I was approaching the situation blinkered, seeing only what was straight ahead of me – Jai on a computer – so I was (metaphorically) beating my head against a wall. Although I still had no idea what to do, as soon as I saw the situation from a broader perspective, I realized I had a choice and I was clear that I didn't want to carry on like that. Although I still didn't know the way forward, I had faith there was another way and, since I was the grown-up, it was probably up to me to change my reaction and let that way emerge. The power of awareness and the perspective that it brings really is wonderful; it never ceases to amaze me.

Stopped in my tracks, I consciously took another step or two back. I stopped trying to fight the situation and acknowledged that I didn't like it, and neither did Jai. I allowed the feelings of guilt, frustration, powerlessness, and inadequacy just to be there, took my attention to them as physical feelings in my body, and made a conscious effort to feel kindness for both myself and Jai within that. Although it was uncomfortable, it immediately felt better than pushing those feelings away or trying to control the source of them – Jai – and they soon lost their power. As someone once quoted to me, all our feelings require of us is to be felt and recognized. Once we do that, they go away 'like creditors who have been paid'. That was certainly my experience. Very soon the closed, narrow, and personal aspect vanished.

With a broader perspective, I saw that we were in a phase of transition, and I was facing the same thing as countless parents of eleven-year-old boys. This wasn't just about me and him. After that, it was easy to tell Jai how I saw things, that I didn't feel critical of him, and that we were both in a time of transition. That gave him space to admit he, too, was fed up with too much computer. We embarked on a joint exploration to find and do things that would still work for us as a family, and ways for Jai to channel his energy and develop skills as a flesh-and-blood human being as well as a character in a complex computer game. One day at the swimming pool, diving down and looking at my son through goggles, I felt a wave of joy as I realized I was literally looking at him from a different perspective, empowered by a wider vision, and therefore able to com-municate love in place of criticism, and that was having an effect. We were all happier and talking to each other again.

This was a very small incident, and in retrospect seems like a fairly brief phase. Yet reflecting on such incidents helps me to place them within a broader context and to build my trust in our innate intuition, to have faith in what emerges if we do pause and step back, seeing what is happening as part of the flow of life, not as fixed or uniquely ours. A difficult phase with children can feel like the sum total of life, and seems never-ending when we are in the thick of it. But if you remember only one teaching that Buddhism offers to us as parents on a path, let it be the fact that everything does change, end, or pass. Nothing is fixed, nothing is permanent. One single mother told me about how interminable the weekends seemed to her with a young child, stretching ahead with ceaseless demands. I remembered feeling the same, felt again the rising sense of panic at how to get through a Saturday. Those times were lots of things, but they were not interminable. They came to an end, and consciously being aware of that prospect can really help bring a broader perspective and open a window to engage differently with the all-too-brief days of Play-Doh and demands to join in with the games.

By the age of 12, Jai was setting his own limits on computer time, and asked me for help in sticking to them. He had taken up martial arts and other new interests, he was spending more time with new friends, and he was generally open and enjoyable to be around. One day, he was jigging around chatting to me in the hall when he suddenly stopped moving, looked me in the eye, and announced happily, 'I like my life!' I think it was coincidence, but it did make me laugh to tell him I had just been editing this part of the book. A few days later the prospect of homework resulted in a considerably less positive outlook along the lines of 'life sucks', reminding me yet again not to allow myself to become fixed about life within my family. But with awareness and perspective comes choice – to react with irritation and carry on feeling overwhelmed or to step back, turning towards the situation rather than standing locked in opposition and allow a different response to emerge. Each time we can turn towards a difficult incident rather than push it away; allowing a creative response to emerge helps to build faith and confidence in the possibilities and choices open to us.

Another way in which Jai has been my great teacher at different phases in his life – and one that you may recognize in your own family life – has been through an ability to hold on to some small injustice for hours, the possibility for enjoyment completely obscured by the dark cloud of a recent experience. It took me a while to realize that in my frustration I can also let myself become drawn into this narrow perspective, so that I, too, become totally caught up in it and quickly degenerate into the did-didn't level of argument. Then we both spiral down, everyone else gets completely ignored, and I am no help at all in enabling Jai to let go and move on.

With children of any age, there is always a challenge to maintain an adult perspective and not behave like a small child or a reactive adolescent. There is so much we can learn from watching our children, but we need that sense of perspective so that we learn from it, not live that way too. And we choose to be the adult not just to avoid being sucked into potentially miserable situations, but within the broader context of our spiritual aspirations, as part of our growth, personally and spiritually, building confidence in ourselves and our ability to bring awareness and perspective to everyday moments, allowing them to teach us yet again how everything changes and everything is so intimately connected.

growing through commitment
Have you ever got up to attend to a crying child in the night whilst unbelievably tired yourself? If you are a parent, you almost certainly have. You may also have longed to just walk away from a toddler having a tantrum and known that you simply can't, or at least you cannot move very far away if it happens to be your toddler. Without negating the fun, the energy, the love, the laughter, and so much more

that we gain through our children, one aspect of parenting is that it requires commitment. We grow and mature through that commitment, by realizing our strength and resources and by persevering with things that are really difficult. Children provide ample opportunities to grow and mature in this way because they can be really difficult, and for most of the time we have to stick with them through the process. This commitment includes signing up for a long haul and committing ourselves as fully and wholeheartedly as possible in each moment.

signing up for the long haul

There is a huge difference between being the adored uncle or aunt when you choose to baby-sit, and a parent who can't get away. One mother with two small boys said she often felt, 'That's it. I've had enough!' They might have done their Play-Doh, sticking, colouring, reading, hide-and-seek, and run out of ideas, her three-year-old was asking, 'What can I do now?' and it was only 10 a.m. She sometimes felt pushed to her limit, with no patience or energy left, and perhaps tearful. Especially when looking after young children, you'll have an insight into the 'no way out' nature of the job. You are tied down, moment by moment, night by night, weekend by weekend. You can't ignore a sick child's needs, even if you're ill yourself, you can't maintain any reasonable expectation of undisturbed sleep when they are tiny, and during the daytime there can be an interminable barrage of demands.

One father described moonlighting after the birth of his first son. He had two jobs. His son woke at six if he was lucky. It was against his nature to jump out of bed and start the day. He wanted space, meditation, and breakfast. But jump he had to. When he got home in the evening, his wife had had a full day of childcare and he would cook and put their son to bed, after which they both collapsed and repeated the procedure the next day. It often feels as if there is a conflict between our needs and the needs of our children, and it is not always easy to respond. Yet it is the same in our spiritual development. It is not always easy, and the aim is to not throw our hands in the air and give up if we find meditation frustrating, self-awareness painful, and being present in each moment simply impossible. As the difficult phases subside and we can breathe more freely, we may notice that we have grown that bit bigger emotionally or spiritually just by staying with the tough times and dealing with each moment as best we could, purely because we had to.

When my ex-husband and I were separating, at first I found it really hard not to get completely caught up and lost in the confusion of emotions, from anger to guilt, self-hatred to dizzy elation and heart-pounding fear, to name just a few. For a while I struggled to give the children the attention they needed, but it happened just as Jai was starting school, and the fear of his having a bad start because of me shocked me into some kind of clarity. I developed a sort of constantly repeating mantra in my head, 'I am going to settle Jai at school.' That is what I decided to focus on, and for several months it kept me grounded and able to touch base when I needed a reminder of what was really important, which was to minimize the disruption and pain to our children. I had no space to think about my spiritual life, let alone consciously try to grow or change, though I did find meditation very helpful indeed, and gave it priority. I was just doing what was needed, trying to settle my son at school and, of course, take good care of my daughter too.

It was an intense time, but once it was over and I had a little bit of space, I realized I had changed and learned a lot. Even though I was just doing what was necessary moment by moment, I came out of it more mature, in ways I noticed through my daily responses, reacting less to small irritations, and finding it easier to see the bigger picture. This seems to be a common experience, and other parents also say they did not realize the progress they were making until they had a short time away from the family, maybe on retreat. Only then, stopping and looking at themselves, did they realize the extent to which they had changed. It is not that immediately after each difficulty we recognize and pride ourselves on having matured, or that we willingly skip out of bed in the night to attend to a sick child because that it will be good for us and help us to grow – at least I don't. But I have an underlying faith built from experience that we do grow by seeing through our commitments, and that benefits our spiritual life too, even if we do not immediately see how.

wholehearted commitment in the moment

Although she was pleased to be having a baby, for one young mother I met her pregnancy was not planned and came at a bad time as far as her work as an artist was concerned. After her son's birth, she felt a lot of grief and resentment. She also developed very bad eczema on her hands, which made washing and caring for the baby difficult and painful. She had to work hard to appreciate mothering as a valuable use of her time, to commit to it day by day rather than seeing it as something to get through in order to get back to artistic creativity and being out in the world. She wanted to do that as soon as she could, to help heal her eczema and because she wanted to start wholeheartedly enjoying looking after her young son.

Commitment is about being completely wholehearted, about putting ourselves and our energy into life moment by moment, fully behind the choices we make and being where we are, whether as a full-time carer or a working parent. It is the same with the spiritual life. It is not simply about accepting a context or path, but committing all of ourselves in every moment. I once saw a meditation retreat advertised as 'total immersion' and wondered what that meant. I think most of my retreats over the years have been total immersion because the time feels so precious, such an opportunity, that I immerse myself totally. Yet the truth is that all of life is so precious, so full of opportunities, that surely this total immersion is what I am aiming for at home too: wholehearted commitment and immersion within life. With that level of commitment, I would be fully present and engaged with what I am doing and who I am with, moment by moment. There is so much that holds us back from that wholeheartedness, yet what better way can there be to spend this precious life?

My image of that wholehearted commitment is a plunge taken with an element of joyful abandon, open to the unknown, with a deep underlying faith that whatever happens, everything will be fine. Yet that is not how I have tended to commit myself in most aspects of life, including spiritually. I had a good image of this when I took my family on a three-day bushcraft course. Apparently, 'survival skills' can keep someone alive for 72 hours, after which time most of us can reasonably expect to be rescued from almost anywhere. After 72 hours, survival depends on 'bushcraft', and you invest time making string from nettle stalk fibres, using glowing embers to burn a bowl shape out of green wood, and other such slow and wonderfully absorbing campfire activities, creating from nature all you need to settle down for a longer spell in the bush. I'd highly recommend it – but that is not the point.

Our 'survival' took place in a none-too-remote woodland near Canterbury. Slightly bizarrely, Elton John played Canterbury on the first night and was at times clearly audible in our temporary wilderness. But that is not the point either. To demonstrate how our intuition can flourish when our brains are encouraged to switch off, we played a number of nature awareness games, including walking blindfold through a wood to locate the source of an intermittent drumbeat. When it was my turn, I made absolutely sure of each step, feeling around in front of me with my feet and thoroughly testing the ground to be sure it would hold me before putting my weight on my front foot, using my outstretched hands to check the space in front of me for branches and tree trunks.

That is exactly how I have been with Buddhism and the Buddhist order of which I am a member. After about ten years there were more leaps of faith, but it took years of testing each step before I trusted it with my weight and before I called myself a Buddhist and embraced spiritual practice as the centre of my life. So what holds us back from wholehearted commitment? Doubt or insecurity, including self-doubt, can keep us sitting on the fence, hedging our bets, holding back, even just a tiny bit, until we are absolutely sure; anything other than plunging headlong into a wholehearted engagement with life. After all, we might make a mistake! One potential pitfall of family life is that it can give us a cast-iron excuse not to commit wholeheartedly in other areas, perhaps on the grounds that we do not have time or space, or we have others to take into account.

But it is not very comfortable on the fence, or holding back from taking the plunge into the unknown. We never know exactly what will happen. You could try taking your attention to your bodily feelings, maybe around your heart area, at a time when you do find yourself holding back, maybe out of doubt or fear, or when bringing such an occasion to mind from memory. You can do the same when you bring to mind a moment of fuller and more wholehearted engagement in life. For me, holding back and resisting is a closed, small feeling, and by definition wholehearted engagement feels just that: bigger, fuller, warmer, and open-hearted. With Buddhism, I felt my way slowly, and I can easily bring to mind many moments of doubt and leaps of faith. Ultimately, we cannot separate wholeheartedly committing ourselves within a seemingly endless weekend with a small child and within our spiritual life; both are a commitment to life. I spend less and less time entertaining doubt and excuses, but I am still learning how to plunge in headfirst with joyful abandon, openness, and faith.

the practice of patience

The wonderful moment when your child first starts to talk is rapidly followed by the realization that, once they start, they don't stop! It can take a while for young children to learn that they do not have to say everything that comes into their heads, even longer to hold emotions. Did you, like many of the parents I interviewed, live with an image of yourself as patient before you had children – and then find that image reduced to shreds within a few months? We may feel our peace shattered as young children are easily distracted or distract us. It can be hard to stay calm, but this is their natural behaviour. We need patience in countless situations, from bedtimes to sibling rivalries, or just getting them out the door with everything they need for school. We often don't get what we want, whether that is sleep, peace, or an uninterrupted conversation. Being at home with children can show us what we can and cannot muster in the way of patience.

We also need patience for our spiritual development, bucketfuls of it. At one level, you may get a glimpse of why patience is so central to Buddhism if you bring to mind the ethical precept that permeates all the others: to avoid causing harm and to act out of kindness and love. You can see that this would be impossible without patience. For example, if someone does something I don't like and I kick out, my intention in that moment is to cause harm. Even if that is just a tiny, fleeting desire to protect myself, or a passing flash of irritation, I am not being kind and I might cause harm. I need to be able to respond with patience if I am to live as much as possible within that first precept.

It can help to remind ourselves of the centrality of patience when we have to take a deep breath to prevent ourselves screaming ourselves hoarse or walking out on someone. We can also place this breath in the wider context of our spiritual aspirations. In addition to improving the immediate situation, it is another small step that enables us to let go into a more creative and fluid way of responding to life, to let go of wanting things to be a certain way, or our need to be right. It is another breath closer to an acceptance of how things actually are, at least for now, towards accepting that our young child will talk almost continuously throughout their waking hours, and doing so genuinely, with patience. This touches on another level of patience altogether. In Buddhism, the term usually translated as patience – *kshanti* – also means acceptance, tolerance, and forbearance, taking the meaning much deeper. What Buddhism can offer within teachings on patience are, in my view at least, some of the most profound and challenging it offers any of us, parents or not.

genuine, patient acceptance

How much time and energy do you spend thinking that situations, other people, and things 'should' be a certain way? When all our children were young, my friends would repeatedly have the same conversations with each other, expressing their frustrations or complaining about their partners' inabilities or the imbalance of responsibility in the home. I am sure I did the same thing. There is so much scope for 'shoulds' about our children, too. People and things are often not as we think they should be, even our children. Every time we say that something should be other than it is, we are arguing rather pointlessly with the ways things actually are, and it can take up a huge amount of time and energy. All my friends who complained about their partners are still with them, and, while there have probably been shifts and compromises, the fundamentals of their relationships remain the same. But they don't complain any more, or very little. What seems to me to have changed is a genuine acceptance of another person for who and how they are, or the balance of who does what at home. This has released energy to be directed elsewhere and opened up more choices.

Many of the more immediate calls on my patience were grown out of years ago, but my children still provide me with a wealth of experience and examples. One is around my and Jai's responses to climate change. After our holiday in Sri Lanka, I took on board much more fully the realities of global warming and the contribution made by aircraft, and made a personal choice to fly much less often. We did lots of fun and interesting things in the following couple of years without having to fly, but Jai has not accepted my decision and has periodic bouts of complaint. Then, after a six-month driving ban taught me how happily I could live without a car, I decided to sell it. Again, Jai was furious. For my part, I can easily get into feeling that the youth of today should care about climate change, and I want them to care, to be aware and interested in the wider world. I can even feel pained and despair about their apparent lack of concern. For Jai, global warming should not be happening and is our generation's fault, and he vehemently believes that he and his generation should not have to compromise or miss out because previous generations messed up. This all adds up to an awful lot of 'shoulds' – and not much room for movement or communication.

I have a choice: to feel helpless, or to accept that Jai's view is what it is, at least for now, and engage with him on that level, opening to more creative responses. A genuine, heartfelt acceptance is completely different from resignation. Instead of defeating us, it removes stress and opens us to more creativity, releasing the energy caught up in beating our head against the wall of how things should be. From a position of greater acceptance, I persuaded him to join Ella and me, with friends and other Buddhists, on a march in London against climate change, which he cheerfully did. We still have huge differences of opinion and I

143

don't always respond well to being challenged, but we do have more common ground and I have more opportunity to influence him and others from a standpoint of acceptance than if we lock horns.

On an even more immediate level, as I write this my children are with their father for the weekend, the sun is shining outside, and several of my friends are on a meditation weekend at the local Buddhist centre. As soon as I veer into wanting to be at the Buddhist centre or in the woods, or anywhere other than where I actually am, I feel a level of discontent, frustration, or pain. Yet when I am just doing what I am doing, accepting the choices I have made, I feel a level of contentment, even happiness. Without acceptance of the way things are, we can expend huge amounts of energy and tie ourselves in knots arguing with how things actually are, or experiencing pain and frustration. Whether this is something major or minor, the approach is the same: Buddhism teaches us that a genuine, patient acceptance of the way things are saves a hell of a lot more energy than fighting, and frees us to direct our energy more effectively.

patience and tolerance

Bring to mind a time when you watched young children play, preferably at pre-school age, at a toddler drop-in perhaps. You probably didn't have to watch them for long to see them hanging onto a toy when it was blatantly obvious that they would have more fun if they were to let go and share, or fighting over something you suspected would be of no interest once won. As you remember watching them, how do you feel? This might be easier thinking about children other than your own. I have reacted with frustration many times on seeing young children locked, if only briefly, in reactions that cause them unnecessary pain. But there are also times when I can watch and just see suffering, and my response is one of patience, not blame or criticism. It is a calm response based on understanding, tolerance, and compassion at witnessing pain, however caused, and knowing that it will pass. This is an insight into another aspect of the Buddhist teachings on patience: a completely genuine tolerance. On a simple level, this means we recognize and empathize with basic human tendencies and respond from that basis.

You have probably had similar responses, quite possibly without identifying them as an insight into the deep tolerance that is part of the teachings offered by Buddhism in relation to patience. For example, you may have comforted your child or one of their friends at a playgroup without feeling even an ounce of blame or anger directed at the tiny perpetrator of their distress. Although not necessarily a conscious thought at the time, that response is based on empathy and understanding: children will be children, that is just how they behave, they are too young to see how pain could so easily be avoided. You might still intervene and try to teach them the more positive consequences of letting go and sharing, but the response is genuine tolerance of the way people can behave. You may also be able to identify similar responses in relation to teenagers, based on a genuine understanding and tolerance of what can lead to pain for themselves and each other. I can easily remember how I felt in my teens, and that can provide me with a source of understanding and empathy if I choose to tap into it.

This insight into tolerance we have access to as parents is incredibly precious. Being able to respond with genuine tolerance and understanding of the way very young children or teenagers behave is an invaluable insight into our natural capacity to respond with tolerance in all situations, based on empathy and understanding of what it is to be human. And it is an insight not only into your capacity or mine, but everyone's. We all have that capacity to feel that way about adults too, even those we see behaving in ways that are clearly destructive or unwise, including those responsible for countries fighting or not sharing resources – just as we respond in our bigger moments to toddlers fighting or not sharing toys. A compassionate response to those who harm children, or the environment, might seem inconceivable, yet this really does strike at the heart of Buddhist teachings on patience.

Taken to this level, patience, tolerance, and forbearance are areas in which Buddhist teachings continue to challenge me more than any other. I don't expect to respond with tolerance and compassion to everyone straight away, but we can try to bring our attention to, and value, the moments of genuine patience and tolerance towards children, identifying what underlies our response, and reflect on how we can start to view what is happening outside our homes with the same level of patience, tolerance, and understanding. We might have moments when we can empathize with people's motivations when they cause harm, and undermine the unhelpful tendency to see goodies and baddies in any situation.

Taken to its highest level, this genuine patience and tolerance enables us to respond with compassion to both the perpetrators and those affected. This is a mind-blowing concept, perhaps, and possibly an unattractive one, but a response of compassion is one of energy and love, liberating us from hatred and freeing us to respond positively and be a force for good in the world.

being patient with ourselves

It is one thing to identify what we want to change about ourselves or our responses to our children, and quite another to put that into practice in times of stress. We need immense patience with ourselves in the spiritual life too. We expect ourselves to change, by chipping away at deeply ingrained ways of being and misunderstandings. This takes time and patience can be a great help, giving ourselves the understanding and leeway to make mistakes, and tolerance towards others. You are as deserving of your empathy, understanding, and acceptance as your children or anyone else.

Buddhism offers a great deal when it comes to the practice of patience, and it also offers an immense challenge and insight into a way of being and responding that is unlikely to manifest overnight. We may have a range of techniques to cultivate patience, such as consciously taking a deep breath or two, counting to ten, or leaving the room to calm down. You might also try recognizing and naming the thoughts or emotions that arise in difficult situations – exasperation, anger, intolerance – without analysing them or going into stories about how they shouldn't be there and you shouldn't be feeling them because you thought you were a tolerant and patient person.

But don't throw the baby out with the bathwater. Sometimes we will manage better than others in responding patiently to sibling rivalry or demands from our children. If we don't succeed, the next opportunity is surely just around the corner. We can always come back to what we are trying to do, to our aspirations for how we want to live. The awareness is there, in any moment, with the next breath. Remaining calm and kind is a moment of practice, and the more we practise something, the better we get. The more we practise patience, whether through pausing to take a breath, or accessing a natural tolerance, the better we become. We are learning. When we don't have access to patience, we can draw on Buddhist teachings on remorse and forgiveness, to forgive ourselves and move on. When we do manage to respond with patience, we can also take a moment to notice how the situation improved, and use that to build our faith in the positive consequences of patience and in our own capacity for acceptance, tolerance, and understanding, both within and beyond our immediate family.

confidence in ourselves and our path

I listened to one mother as she wondered aloud what would happen when she finally ran out of the energy and love she needed in meeting her daughter's demands at the end of a long day. She wondered whether she would find herself turning inside out as she dug deeper to find those resources. Another mother talked about facing what to do when her young teenage daughter hadn't come home by two o'clock in the morning. I have also felt rising panic at times, fear that I simply would not be able to hold it together as a single mother with a mortgage to pay, afraid that I wouldn't be able to cope. That is not a feeling I am used to. In my working life, I feel completely confident most of the time. Work-wise, I have been doing my present job for so long that I am confident that whatever question someone asks, however negative, I will be able to deal with it. I don't feel that to nearly the same extent as a parent.

Even a single generation ago, there were accepted ways to raise children in various cultures. There was one way that was perceived to be right, and certain things you should or should not do. We now live in a very different situation. In much of the UK there is a tremendous mix of cultures, many people writing about how to raise children, trends, fashions, and contradictory theories. This can contribute to a lack of confidence in ourselves as parents, giving an impression that other people know the right way and we do not. During the course of one day, situations will arise in which we simply do not know, or don't feel confident, what our response should be. We may doubt ourselves or be unable to decide between conflicting options.

Buddhism teaches that this very unknowing is a positive opportunity, and encourages us to view such experiences as an inevitable aspect of the way things are, of the inter-connections, change, and flow of life. We cannot know or control everything; we will always meet the unknown eventually. If we try to make things safe and fixed and pre-dictable, we are living an illusion and missing out on the potential for growth that comes with facing those moments of unknowing. So when we face the emotions and thoughts that can rush in while we are outside our comfort zone, Buddhism encourages us to recognize that and open to it, trying to stay with 'I don't know what to do,' or 'I don't know if I can cope,' and not panic, close down, or rush to find a solution. As with other emotions or sources of pain and discomfort, a helpful way to open to them is to consciously direct your attention to what is happening in your body, notice any feelings of panic or closing off in the pit of your stomach and, if possible, engage your curiosity: isn't it interesting that moving beyond what we are sure we can cope with can give rise to such powerful responses?

By allowing ourselves to sit with this unknowing, we open to a much deeper level of confidence, which is available to all of us all the time, a deep underlying sanity or welling up of a depth of confidence that is not conditional on having been here before or worked in some area for many years. If we allow ourselves to move beyond the narrow, condi-tional confidence, we can touch a level where we have faith in ourselves, not because of our attributes or skills, but sim-ply because this basic sanity exists as a bottom line, when we allow ourselves to touch it. It is not uniquely ours, developed through years of hard work; it is a level of confi-dence that is unconditional, and through it we tap into far greater creativity and intuition than tend to be available to us when we try to stay within our boundaries and abilities.

The mother who feared she could not find the resources she needed was not actually inside out. She had always managed at some level. The mother whose teenage daugh-ter was still out at 2 a.m. did what she could, then went to bed. When I confided to a Buddhist teacher about my ris-ing panic at being unable to cope, her advice to me was, 'Don't panic.' She told me that all I really needed – all any of us really need – is confidence. By going to the edge and beyond what we think we can cope with, and not closing down or running away, we are less dependent on firm ground under our feet, more able to operate in the unknown, more in touch with the flow of life, and we can tap into a deeper confidence.

Maybe, then, we do not even need to know what a spiritual path for parents is or how to tread it. We need confidence – faith – that embracing the countless opportunities to open to the life presented by our children and parenting are enough. With a wholehearted engagement with all of life, the rest will unfold.

conclusion: tools and tips

the breath as a way to awareness

Finding that I continue to do things that I know are unhelpful can be infuriating. I suspect this is a familiar experience. It could be something as small as picking at food while waiting for the kettle to boil, working too late at night, screaming at my children, or postponing meditation or the gym. Without awareness, we might resolve to change countless times, but still continue our habits. I have learned the consequences of this again and again: I put on weight through snacking, walk around like a zombie the day after working late, or feel guilty or horribly busy. I know I don't like these things, and that zombies do not make very good parents, yet it is extremely difficult to change our behaviour. Just knowing that I need to sleep more, snack less, scream less, and meditate every day is not enough. Neither is will-power, not in the long term. In order to change, we need awareness.

Our breath is the simplest and most immediate way to awareness. It is always available to us. It is never too late to use it. We can be completely cut off from ourselves for hours, days, weeks, or months, but the very next breath is always an opportunity to come back to awareness of yourself wherever you are and whatever you are doing. Taking your attention to your breath is an excellent way to make the short but crucial transition between all your attention being in your head with your thoughts, and directing attention into the body, below the neck. The breath very conveniently travels from our heads down to the area around our hearts, so if we consciously place our attention on our breath and follow its movement down, the breath gently carries our awareness into our bodies. Try following at least three consecutive breaths and see what difference it makes to your immediate experience.

three-minute playground meditation

I learned the three-minute breathing space on a mindfulness-based stress-reduction course, and offer it here as tool you can use. Try doing it three times a day for at least a couple of weeks, so that it becomes a familiar and accessible technique which you can then use when you need or want it – or when you remember. It involves three short stages, which I picture as a funnel bringing our broad awareness down to a focused awareness on the breath, then allowing it to expand out again.

First, bring yourself into the present moment by adopting an upright and dignified posture, and close your eyes. Bring your attention to what is going on in your mind and body, maybe by deliberately asking yourself, 'What is my experience right now? What thoughts are there? What feelings and bodily sensations?' It can be helpful to name the experiences, for example 'tiredness round my eyes' or 'self-critical thought' or 'anxiety about my child'. As best you can, just become aware of and acknowledge all that is going on, even if you don't like it or don't want it. There is no need to try to change it. Just be aware of it.

Secondly, gently direct attention to your breath. Follow the breath all the way in and all the way out again. To help maintain attention on your breathing, it can help to say to yourself, 'breathing in, breathing out,' or to count each breath. It is amazing how our minds will resist taking a back seat even for a minute, rushing in with ever more urgent or engaging thoughts. That is not wrong or a failure; it is just what minds do. Just note these thoughts and gently bring your attention back to your breath.

Thirdly, after a few breaths, broaden out your awareness, bringing attention to the physical sensations in your body, perhaps some tension in your shoulders, the warmth of the sun of your face, tiredness in your legs, or feeling hot or cold somewhere. Become aware of your posture and facial expression, and relax them if necessary. Whatever sensations you find, carry on breathing with awareness, and allow the awareness to include any tension or resistance, opening to include and embrace it. It may help to say in your mind, 'It's OK, whatever it is, it's OK.'

I call this the playground meditation because I have spent quite a lot of time in playgrounds over the years, waiting for my children at school or in parks. Such occasions can be good opportunities to maintain a social life and adult communication, but when you are alone they present an excellent opportunity to practise the three-minute meditation. Experiment with different places and times. It does work best if you can close your eyes, but neither this nor the timing is not crucial. Feel free to read 'short' instead of three-minute, and do it for longer if you can. Then notice how you feel and respond as your child rushes up, or you have to find them to take them home. Try to stay in contact with the expanded awareness and stillness you can access in this meditation. If you notice any increased intensity or calm, store that experience consciously – it might make it that bit easier to do the three-minute meditation next time.

meditating for longer
I don't think I could have survived without meditation. Meditation has been many things for me over the years, sometimes overtly nourishing, blissful, or insightful, at other times more of a routine I continue out of faith that it helps. Whatever my immediate experience, I cannot recommend it highly enough. I don't know how anyone really survives without meditation, and the exercises described above are more effective when backed by regular longer

periods of meditation. One father told me, 'Meditation reaches the parts that other techniques cannot reach in terms of being a calm parent. It makes shed-loads of difference.' He said that if he had made space to meditate in the morning, he was far better with his children if they were naughty. If he argued with his wife, he knew that if he went upstairs and meditated he might be furious to start with, but after half an hour he could come downstairs wanting to give her a hug. As well as calmness, meditation gave him the space and perspective to tap into what was important, and let go of petty preoccupations.

It was meditation that first attracted me to Buddhism, and it became my route towards becoming a Buddhist. There is no being good or bad at it. Anyone can meditate, though people's experiences in meditation vary. It is beyond the scope of this book to teach meditation more fully, but there are many books that do so extremely well. (Some are included in list at the end of this book.) Some of the most well-known meditation techniques use the breath as an anchor and a way to develop awareness. Doing twenty or forty minutes of meditation on a regular basis also builds our ability to bring awareness to ourselves when we are under pressure, and to live more of our lives in our bodies, not just in our minds. We can set up conditions to make it easier than in a playground, providing more space to learn and explore what awareness can actually feel like. And if we can learn in meditation what it feels like to be aware of everything, with some space in which to look at it, we can do that more easily at other times too.

joining a class or retreat

I used to go to my local Buddhist centre every Thursday evening. For the first year or two, there was a regular pattern to my week. Meditating with others and talking about meditation on a Thursday gave me a boost, and I would enthusiastically meditate on Friday, Saturday, probably

Sunday, maybe Monday, and almost certainly not Tuesday. Then I'd go back on Thursday and get another boost. After a couple of months, I might start missing a few Thursdays or even stop meditating completely. Then I would go on a meditation retreat, either for a weekend or whole week, and all my motivation and energy would come flooding back and I'd start again.

I am no longer dependent on a weekly class, or even retreats, to keep going with meditation. After many years I have enough faith built on direct experience to keep going by myself, though even now I still have days when I do not meditate. However, I still love meditating with others, and spending time with people who also meditate. In Buddhism, the community of followers of the Buddha has always been important for learning from others and mutual support between peers. I have heard many people say the same, about how different they find it to meditate in a group, and how much it helps their practice during the week. You might not live near somewhere with meditation classes or groups, or it might not appeal to you, but it is a tool I would recommend exploring if possible.

transforming daily tasks

Try bringing your awareness to a particular task for two or three weeks at a time. In a similar way to the mother I mentioned in Chapter 2, who transformed her experience of ironing, you could pick a simple routine task that you usually perform without much awareness. Avoid tasks you really dislike. It is best to begin with a neutral or dull task. Resolve to bring your attention to it for a prescribed period of time, and to carry it out as an integral part of your spiritual journey, as wholeheartedly as possible and in touch with love and compassion.

I have a clear memory of chopping lots of vegetables on a recent retreat. Because I had been meditating and we were in silence, I was more aware and it was an intensely pleasurable experience, full of colours, textures, and smells, combined with simple movements, and my task was transformed into delight in the knowledge that I was preparing food for others.

When you start your chosen task, check your posture, aiming for the upright and dignified posture that is a good basis for meditation, checking that you are comfortable and grounded. Try using your breath to bring attention to your body and keep your attention in your body as you carry out the task. Notice the smells and colours and textures. Maintain awareness of the breath. You need not slow down or do anything else differently.

With time, your experience of the task will change. As well as making it more pleasant, you will start to shift your habitual feelings about that particular task. This can help build faith that it is possible to change. After a few weeks of consciously bringing attention to a task and carrying it out with awareness and love, our habits, attitudes, and behaviours really can be transformed. If we can change our experience of one task through awareness, we can change our experience of everything, little by little. The Buddhist poet, Dogen, likened this to walking in a fine misty rain until we realize we are wet through. We do little things that accumulate, and one day we realize we are soaked, that the compartments we may have had between what is 'spiritual' and what is not have been dissolved, and our life is our spiritual practice.

the spiritual path is ongoing

Throughout the process of writing this book I have had a song line in my head, 'It's not what you do but the way that you do it – that's what gets results.' You might recognize it. There are opportunities and challenges in all lifestyles, including raising a family. What is important is how we are within the context in which we live; that we live as best we can with awareness and alive to our heart connection with our spiritual aspirations. What I have attempted to do in this book is highlight the opportunities that are the gifts of being a parent and draw on Buddhist teachings to explore how we can embrace those opportunities to help us to grow. I have tried to bring a wealth of gifts into these pages, from the heart opening that can give us a glimpse of our capacity to love, to the mirror turned to reflect both the noble and the inconsistent in our behaviour. Within the richness of opportunity to practise generosity and patience, for example, I have suggested ways in which we can expand beyond our family to allow our experiences to permeate all other aspects of how we are in the world. I have also highlighted some inherent difficulties, where family life can close us down instead of open us up, and explored ways we can turn towards them so that they, too, become opportunities for growth.

Through writing this book, I have experienced – not for the first time – what a difference it makes to be wholehearted in what we do and how we do it. The heightened awareness of love, patience, generosity, and so much more that I have felt while writing, transformed my experience and my effect on my family and the world around me. Simply bringing attention to these areas can, in itself, be powerfully transformative. This is a lesson I have learned time and time again. I can still so easily lose awareness, or feel swamped by the demands of the moment to maintain my perspective or connection, but then I remember, and bring myself back with the next breath. You, too, might well know what helps you maintain your connection with something bigger and higher, and then not always do it. But where we place our attention has an enormous effect, and each time we do remember, and respond with kindness and understanding, we see the consequences, and that can reinforce our choices for next time. I have faith that reading this book will, at the very least, have brought your attention to your desire to grow spiritually, and that alone will have an effect.

I said in the introduction that this book was an important part of my exploration of how to lead a spiritual life while raising children, how to grow as my children grow. It became a more important part than I could possibly have imagined, and that exploration is definitely ongoing. Returning to successive drafts, I find that what I said about my children has become a thing of the past, and now, reaching the end of the book, I am left with a strong image of Jai and Ella as ungraspable, of a shifting unpredictability and flow. The anxieties that hold my attention today are new again, as are moments that make my heart lift and sing, and the exasperation.

So much is unknown, there is so much I simply cannot be sure about or guarantee. For all I have written, there are still many times when I wish I could know something for sure. Yet I also have a rather beautiful if intangible sense of all of life with the same flow, the same stubborn refusal to be fixed. And I have the same impression of my spiritual journey, a sense of something ungraspable, of a shifting and flowing, and so very much that is unknown and unknowable. All I do know is that I have a renewed clarity, openness, and faith in embracing whatever comes as best I can. I wish you well and happy in your own explorations.

notes

1 The *Metta Sutta*. This discourse is found twice in the Buddhist scriptures, at *Sutta Nipata* i.8, and also at *Khuddakapatha* 9.

2 Generosity is the first of the six perfections. It is through perfecting these qualities that the Bodhisattva – the ideal Buddhist – gains Enlightenment, or spiritual perfection, and so can we. These are usually listed as generosity, ethical discipline, patience, enthusiastic effort, concentration, and wisdom.

Several chapters of this book relate directly to the six perfections. Chapter 2 explores how to transform giving into generosity, ethical discipline is the subject of Chapter 5, patience is covered in Chapter 7, and wisdom is the subject of Chapter 4. The need for enthusiastic effort and concentration – awareness – is emphasized throughout.

3 *Itivuttaka* 26.

4 *Sallatha Sutta, Samyutta Nikaya* 36.8 (iv.208).

5 Sangharakshita, *Buddha Mind*, Windhorse Publications, 2001.

6 This formula occurs many times in the Buddhist scriptures, for example at *Majjhima Nikaya* ii.32 and *Samyutta Nikaya* ii.28.

7 The noble eightfold path is one of the best-known Buddhist teachings. The eight stages of the path are perfect vision, perfect emotion, perfect speech, perfect action, perfect livelihood, perfect effort, perfect awareness, and perfect *samadhi* (higher concentration).

All these stages are touched on within the context of raising children. Perfect vision is what gets us started in the first place.

Perfect emotion concerns the process of moving from simply knowing what we should do, or intellectual understanding of a teaching, to actually changing how we respond, as discussed throughout this book but especially in the chapters on self-awareness and ethics. Perfect speech is the fourth of the five precepts touched on in the chapter on ethics, and perfect action includes the principles and practice of ethics, covered in more depth in the same chapter.

Perfect livelihood is the aspect that looks beyond our personal transformation, and is discussed in terms of the positive effect of our practice both within and beyond our family. One aspect of the sixth stage – perfect effort – is the energy we need to keep us going, as discussed in Chapter 6 when looking at how being with children can help with our energy and vitality. It is also a reminder to keep up our spiritual practice. The role of awareness, the seventh stage, is emphasized throughout this book as fundamental to spiritual development.

The final stage of the path – perfect *samadhi* – is touched upon in relation to meditation, but it can be taken to mean higher concentration or one-pointedness as Enlightenment, representing the fruition of the whole path, which I have not attempted to discuss in any detail.

7 *Udana* i.10.

bibliography

I have found the following useful in writing this book.
Ancient Wisdom, Modern World: Ethics for the New Millennium,
   by the Dalai Lama, Abacus, 2001.
Everyday Blessings: The Inner Work of Mindful Parenting,
   by Myla and Jon Kabat-Zinn, MJF Books, 2000.
Living with Awareness,
   by Sangharakshita, Windhorse Publications, 2003.
Lovingkindness: The Revolutionary Art of Happiness,
   by Sharon Salzberg, Shambhala Publications, 2003.
A Survey of Buddhism,
   by Sangharakshita, Windhorse Publications, 2001.
*Vision and Transformation: An Introduction to the Buddha's Noble
   Eightfold Path*,
   by Sangharakshita, Windhorse Publications, 1999.
What is the Dharma? The Essential Teachings of the Buddha,
   by Sangharakshita, Windhorse Publications, 1998.
Writing Your Way,
   by Manjusvara, Windhorse Publications, 2005.

Meditation is best taught by a personal teacher, but there are
   several useful books available, including the following.
Change Your Mind,
   by Paramananda, Windhorse Publications, 1996.
Breath by Breath,
   by Larry Rosenberg, Shambhala Publications, 2004.
Wildmind: A Step-by-Step Guide to Meditation,
   by Bodhipaksa, Windhorse Publications, 2003.
Miracle of Mindfulness: A Manual on Meditation,
   by Thich Nhat Hanh, Beacon Press, 1987.
Mindfulness of Breathing and *Body Scan* CDs,
   by Sona and Vidyamala, Breathworks, 2004.

The windhorse symbolizes the energy of the Enlightened mind carrying the truth of the Buddha's teachings to all corners of the world. On its back the windhorse bears three jewels: a brilliant gold jewel represents the Buddha, the ideal of Enlightenment, a sparkling blue jewel represents the teachings of the Buddha, the Dharma, and a glowing red jewel, the community of the Buddha's enlightened followers, the Sangha. Windhorse Publications, through the medium of books, similarly takes these three jewels out to the world.

Windhorse Publications is a Buddhist publishing house, staffed by practising Buddhists. We place great emphasis on producing books of high quality, accessible and relevant to those interested in Buddhism at whatever level. Drawing on the whole range of the Buddhist tradition, our books include translations of traditional texts, commentaries, books that make links with Western culture and ways of life, biographies of Buddhists, and works on meditation.

As a charitable institution we welcome donations to help us continue our work. We also welcome manuscripts on aspects of Buddhism or meditation. For orders and catalogues log on to www.windhorsepublications.com or contact:

Windhorse Publications	Consortium	Windhorse Books
11 Park Road	1045 Westgate Drive	PO Box 574
Birmingham	St Paul MN 55114	Newtown NSW 2042
B13 8AB	USA	Australia
UK		

Windhorse Publications is an arm of the Friends of the Western Buddhist Order, which has more than sixty centres on four continents. Through these centres, members of the Western Buddhist Order offer regular programmes of events for the general public and for more experienced students. These include meditation classes, public talks, study on Buddhist themes and texts, and bodywork classes such as t'ai chi, yoga, and massage. The FWBO also runs several retreat centres and the Karuna Trust, a fundraising charity that supports social welfare projects in the slums and villages of India.

Many FWBO centres have residential spiritual communities and ethical businesses associated with them. Arts activities are encouraged too, as is the development of strong bonds of friendship between people who share the same ideals. In this way the FWBO is developing a unique approach to Buddhism, not simply as a set of techniques, but as a creatively directed way of life for people living in the modern world.

If you would like more information about the FWBO please visit the website at www.fwbo.org or write to:

London Buddhist Centre	Aryaloka	Sydney Buddhist Centre
51 Roman Road	14 Heartwood Circle	24 Enmore Road
London	Newmarket NH 03857	Newtown NSW 2042
E2 0HU	USA	Australia
UK		

ALSO FROM WINDHORSE PUBLICATIONS

Buddhism: Tools for Living Your Life

by Vajragupta

This book is a guide for those seeking a meaningful spiritual path while living everyday lives full of families, work, and friends. Vajragupta provides clear explanations of Buddhist teachings and guidance applying these to enrich our busy and complex lives.

The personal stories, exercises, reflections, and questions in this book help transform Buddhist practice into more than a fine set of ideals. They make the path of ethics, meditation, and wisdom a tangible part of our lives.

> In this book I have attempted to convey a feeling for what a 'Buddhist life' might be like – the underlying flavour, or ethos, of such a life. I hope I have made it clear that this way of life is possible for anyone – whatever their background and experience. My aim is to make the teachings as accessible and relevant as possible, and to give you some 'tools' with which to live a spiritual life.

"I'm very pleased that someone has finally written this book! At last, a real 'toolkit' for living a Buddhist life. His practical suggestions are hard to resist!"

Saddhanandi, Chair of Taraloka, named Retreat Centre of the Year 2006 by *The Good Retreat Guide*

192 pages
ISBN 9781 899579 74 7
£10.99/$16.95/€16.95

Detox Your Heart

by Valerie Mason-John

Have you ever felt angry, resentful or even revengeful? The author, Valerie Mason-John, draws on her own life, personal stories, and current work as an anger management trainer to explore why we can experience such emotions and how we can transform toxins like anger, hatred, and fear.

Our ability to love and be open is often blocked by toxins inside the heart – jealousy, hatred, anger, prejudice, fear, resentment. With short exercises drawing on Buddhist teachings that encourage pausing, connecting, feeling, and loving, *Detox Your Heart* helps us to renew and open our heart.

I'm generally not a fan of self-help manuals, but this is something different.... This is an author passing on the wisdom of hard experience and showing there is a way to get yourself back on track. Her honesty, warmth, and humanity are a precious and all too rare commodity. **Jenni Murray**, BBC's Women's Hour

Offers readers both the inspiration and the insight to work on themselves.
Christopher Titmuss, author of *Transforming Our Terror*

This is a book full of heart which explores with compassion the many layers of human emotions. **Jackee Holder**, author of *Soul Purpose*

208 pages
ISBN 9781 899579 65 5
£9.99/$13.95/€13.95

THE ART OF MEDITATION

The Breath

by Vessantara

The breath: always with us, necessary to our very existence, but often unnoticed. Yet giving it attention can transform our lives.

This is a very useful combination of practical instruction on the mindfulness of breathing with much broader lessons on where the breath can lead us. Vessantara, a meditator of many years experience, offers us:

* Clear instruction on how to meditate on the breath
* Practical ways to integrate meditation into our lives
* Suggestions for deepening calm and concentration
* Advice on how to let go and dive into experience
* Insights into the lessons of the breath

The Breath returns us again and again to the fundamental and precious experience of being alive.

144 pages
ISBN 9781 899579 69 3
£6.99/$10.95/€10.95

The Heart

by Vessantara

The Heart offers ways to discover your emotional potential through an exploration of the practice of loving-kindness meditation.

Vessantara has practised this meditation for over thirty years. Here he shares his experience, gently encouraging us to unlock what is in our hearts and helping us to gain greater enjoyment from life. Among other benefits, using the exercises and meditations in this book you can:

* Increase your emotional awareness
* Feel more at ease with yourself
* Become kinder and more open-hearted
* Discover how to be more patient
* Engage more spontaneously with life.

The Heart provides clear instruction and helpful suggestions for those new to meditation as well as more experienced practitioners.

176 pages
ISBN 9781 899579 71 6
£6.99/$10.95/€10.95

The art of meditation series continues with *The Body*, available late 2007.

WHAT BUDDHISM CAN OFFER

To survive the twenty-first century we need to develop new ways of responding to each other and the planet, discover new paths to wisdom, combined with a growing sense of awareness of the consequences of our actions.

A new series from Windhorse Publications seeks to explore the fruits of western exploration of Buddhism to see what practical contribution it can make to our lives. In the books in this series we discover how Buddhist practices and teachings can help us live life more fully in the twenty-first century – whether we are Buddhist or not.

Suitable for people of any faith – or no faith – each book looks at a universal life issue and offers tools for change and growth. Drawing on the experiences of a variety of people, these books share what works, and how, in an engaging and practical way.

The series may cover topics as diverse as

* Parenting
* Communication
* Working with physical pain
* Ageing
* Coping with stress and anxiety